WOODTURNING
PATTERNS

80+ Designs for the Workshop, Garden,
and Every Room in the House

This book is dedicated to Dave Richards and Tim Killen,
good friends and mentors, and especially to my wonderful
wife, Katherine Foran. My thanks also go to Matthew Teague
and Paul McGahren, of Spring House Press, for giving me
the opportunity to produce this book.

Publisher: Paul McGahren
Editorial Director: Matthew Teague
Copy Editor: Kerri Grzybicki
Design and Layout: Michael Douglas
Illustration: David Heim

Spring House Press
3613 Brush Hill Court
Nashville, TN 37216
ISBN: 978-1-940611-69-3

Library of Congress Control Number: 2017937431
Printed in China
First Printing: July 2017

Note: The following list contains names used in *Woodturning Patterns*
that may be registered with the United States Copyright Office:
American Association of Woodturners; *American Woodturner;* Berea College;
Cheerios; Croquet Association; CrushGrind; *Fargo; Heirloom Furniture;*
Major League Baseball; *Shameless;* Showtime; Spectraply.

The information in this book is given in good faith; however, no warranty is given,
nor are results guaranteed. Woodworking is inherently dangerous. Your safety is
your responsibility. Neither Spring House Press nor the authors assume any
responsibility for any injuries or accidents.

To learn more about Spring House Press books, or to find a retailer near you,
email info@springhousepress.com or visit us at www.springhousepress.com.

WOODTURNING
PATTERNS

80+ Designs for the Workshop, Garden,
and Every Room in the House

WRITTEN AND ILLUSTRATED BY
DAVID HEIM

SPRING HOUSE PRESS

CONTENTS

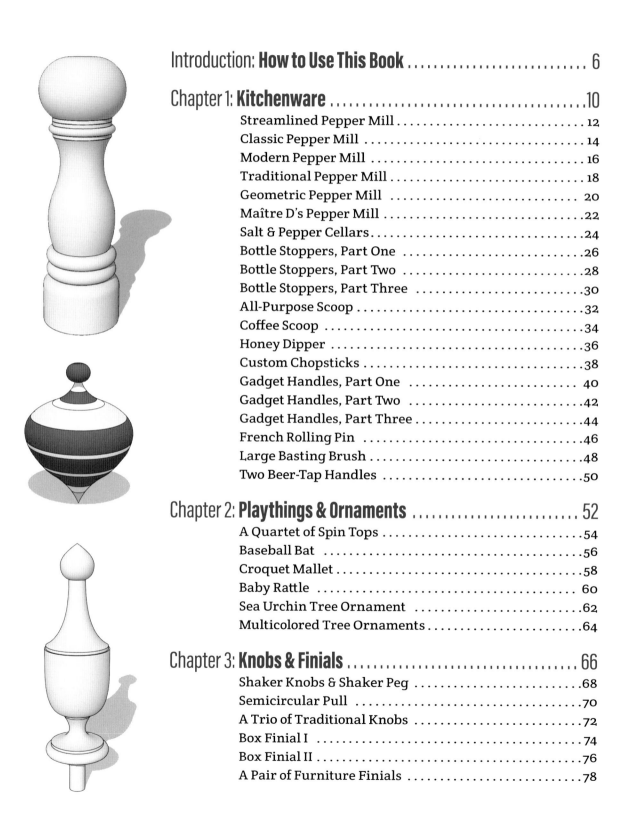

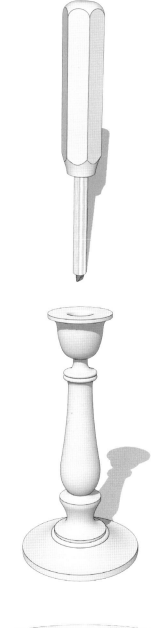

INTRODUCTION

How to Use This Book

Woodturning is like music. The composer uses a small number of tones to create infinite melodies, and the turner uses four basic cuts—a bead, a cove, a fillet, and a V—to create infinitely varied shapes. So you can think of this book as a songbook for the lathe—a few melodies to help you get started.

This book also continues a tradition that harks back at least to the time of the American Revolution. For more than two hundred years, house-builders, carpenters, and cabinetmakers have used pattern books to copy or adapt molding profiles, baseboard designs, window-frame parts, and a variety of other pieces. Using a pattern saves time and helps ensure that you will get the results you want.

If you copy any of these patterns exactly, you can't go wrong. The patterns provide all the necessary dimensions, which you can transfer directly to the wood. Or, you can copy a pattern, cut out the profile, and use it as a template while you turn. In most cases, the patterns are full-size, but a few of the larger ones are shown three-quarter, half, or even one-quarter size. Many of the patterns are taken or adapted from classic objects and pieces of furniture, and the rest are original designs. But don't be afraid to use these patterns as a starting point for your own turning design.

For a complicated pattern, practice a few times, using pine, poplar, or fir. Then, when you think you have it, switch to what a friend of mine calls "the pretty wood."

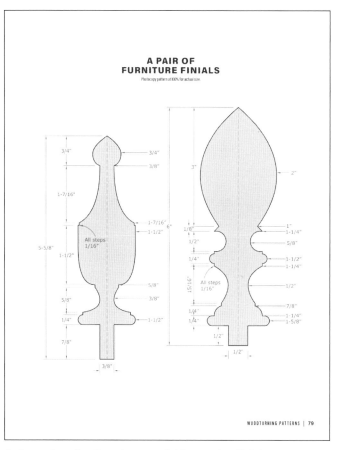

A dimensioned pattern is essential for turning finials.

Transfer critical dimesions from the pattern directly onto the turning blank. These key points identify transitions from straight to round as well as the size at each point.

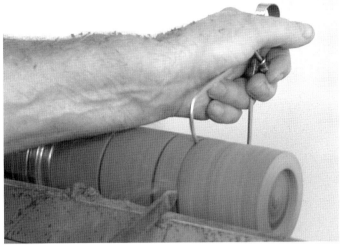

Use calipers in conjunction with a parting tool to turn the key diameters. Once those areas are established, you can go on to shape beads, coves, fillets, and tapers.

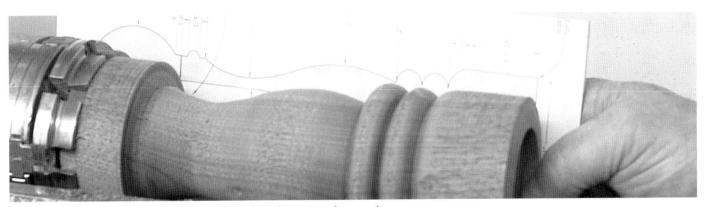

As the turning progresses, check your work against the pattern frequently.

Woodturning Basics

There are two types of woodturning. With **spindle** turning, the wood is oriented so that the grain runs parallel to the lathe bed. Legs, spindles, balusters, and candlesticks are all examples of spindle turning. With **faceplate** turning, the wood is oriented so that the grain runs perpendicular to the lathe bed. Bowls, vases, and vessels are usually done as faceplate turnings, but you can also make those pieces with the wood oriented on the lathe like a spindle.

Always mount the wood securely on the lathe. For spindle turning, this usually means holding it between centers; that is, with a spur or stebcenter at the headstock and a cone or cup center at the tailstock, with the tailstock advanced to squeeze the wood between those centers. For faceplate work, you can screw a faceplate to the wood, or glue a block of scrap to the wood and grip the scrap with a faceplate or a scroll chuck. You can also use a screw chuck, which holds the wood on a thick screw driven into the center of the bowl blank.

Begin any turning by making the blank of wood round. For spindle turning, do that with a spindle roughing gouge. For faceplate work, use a bowl gouge. This is the woodturning equivalent of using a jointer and planer to prepare flat stock.

With the wood trued up, use a pencil to lay out the key points of the turning. That's where the patterns in this book come into play.

Spindle Turning: Diameters Are Key

The time-honored way to copy a spindle turning is to rely on key diameters and a story stick (sometimes called a preacher). Each pattern in this book includes the length of the turning and the diameters at key points, such as the widest and narrowest parts of the shape, as well as the thickness of beads and flat transition points.

If you want to make a single copy of a pattern, transfer the measurements directly to the wood. If you want multiple copies, copy the pattern and glue the copy to a piece of thick cardboard or 1/8-in. plywood to make the story stick. Draw

Using a screw chuck, shown here as part of a larger scroll chuck, is an easy way to secure bowl blank as you turn the outside.

Wiith the outside shaped, turn the bowl around and hold the foot in a scroll chuck to shape the interior.

lines at the key-diameter points from the edge of the pattern to the edge of the plywood, then lay the story stick on the wood and mark the key diameter points. This method allows you to begin each turning with identical dimensions.

Set a pair of calipers to the size of each key diameter. If you're making just one turning, you can reset one pair of calipers. For multiple turnings, however, it's much easier to use a different pair of calipers for each diameter.

Use a parting tool to turn grooves in the blank down to the size of each key diameter. Once you've begun a groove, hold the calipers in it and keep turning until the instant the calipers slip over the wood.

With those diameters established, switch to a spindle gouge, skew chisel, or bedan and begin cutting the beads and coves that make up the shape. Stop frequently and check your work against the pattern.

Repeat the process for each turning you need to make. Pay particular attention to the lengths of the turnings, keeping them as uniform as possible. The eye can quickly pick up small variations in length. Keep widths as uniform as you can, but don't worry too much if one turning is slightly different from the others; the eye is pretty forgiving of differences in width. That said, it's always a good idea to make one extra turning, just in case.

Faceplate Turning: Set a Pattern

These days, most bowls and vessels are turned in this sequence:

One. Hold the work with a faceplate or a screw chuck and shape the outside, including a tenon or recess for the jaws of a scroll chuck. Gauge the progress of the work by holding the pattern close to the turning. For a single turning, just get the shape of the turning as close as you can to the pattern. If you're making multiples, copy the pattern and paste it to heavy cardboard or 1/8 in. plywood. Cut out the profile to use as a reference.

Two. Remove the work from the faceplate or screw chuck. Screw the scroll chuck onto the lathe's headstock spindle and hold the foot of the piece in the chuck. Make sure the wood still runs true, reshaping it as needed. Shape the inside, making sure that the curve on the inside of the bowl parallels the outside curve. You can use calipers, but your fingers are just as good.

Three. This step is optional; if you've shaped the foot of the bowl as you like in step one, there's no need for this step. Remove the bowl again. Attach a chunk of scrap to a faceplate and turn a jam chuck—a shape that the bowl will fit over snugly. Push the bowl onto the jam chuck and tweak its position as needed so it runs true. Do the final shaping on the foot of the bowl.

Tips for Large or Deep Turnings

You can make many faceplate turnings or spindles from a single piece of wood. But for some work, such as a lamp base, it may be easier and more economical to glue up a blank from several pieces of wood. You can either stack layers of thin

When shaping a bowl, work from the rim of the toward the center and down to the foot.

You can use special calipers (or your fingers) to gauge the uniformity of the bowl's wall thickness.

stock or glue up rings composed of several wedge-shaped pieces. Do the math to figure out the miter angle for the wedges: 36° for five pieces, 30° for six pieces, and so on.

I use large hose clamps to hold the pieces together for a dry fit and glue-up. (If the pieces don't fit together snugly, run the edges along a belt or disc sander to true them up). Add a solid piece at one end for the base; or, if you also want a solid rim, add pieces at both ends.

Tips for Goblets and Such

To make something that's wide at the ends but narrow in the middle—a candlestick, for example—turn the base separately. Glue the pieces together when you have shaped and sanded them.

When you turn something long and thin, you may need to support it in the middle with a lathe accessory known as a steady rest. You can buy one or make your own from scrap plywood and recycled inline-skate wheels and bearings; just search the Internet for "steady rest plans." For small, thin turnings, try supporting the work with a web of string. Search the Internet for "string steady rest" to learn how to weave that web.

Dry Wood or Green?

Most of the patterns in this book are best made with dry wood. If you work with freshly cut, or green, wood, there's a good chance the piece will shrink, split, or go out of round as it loses moisture.

You can use green wood, but you will have to be patient. Turn the piece, but leave it larger than its finished

To finish a bowl's foot, you often need to make a jam chuck, so named because you jam the bowl over it.

dimensions. For a bowl, leave the wall and base at least an inch thick; having a uniform thickness throughout is more important than the actual measurement. For a spindle, turn the blank round but don't do any further shaping.

Wrap the piece in a double layer of brown-paper bags to moderate the rate of moisture loss. Then wait. If you can, weigh the piece every week or so. When the weight stabilizes, take it out of the bags and put it back on the lathe to be turned again.

PATTERNS

CHAPTER

1

Kitchenware

There is a seemingly endless collection of kits for turned kitchenware: handles for pizza cutters, cheese slicers, ice-cream scoops, bottle stoppers, and vegetable peelers. Add to that kits for pepper mills and beer taps. What all those projects have in common is simplicity: The setup at the lathe is quick and easy, and the turning is simple even for a beginner. The finished pieces always make welcome gifts.

You'll find patterns for all those kit handles in this chapter, plus patterns for a rolling pin, chopsticks, a honey dipper, and small scoops.

Most of these projects require very little wood, so you can splurge on exotic (i.e., expensive) species that have outstanding grain and figure. Jump in and outfit your kitchen with useful and beautiful handmade turnings.

Kitchenware

STREAMLINED PEPPER MILL

This simple but practical shape is designed to fit smoothly in your hand, as well as look elegant on a kitchen counter or dining table. Included are patterns both for 10-in. CrushGrind and traditional pepper mill mechanisms. (Note: Some CrushGrind kits require a notch to be shaped in the base to hold locking tabs on the grinding mechanism.) If you choose to use a traditional mechanism, drill holes as shown in the right-hand pattern.

Pepper mill kits typically come with instructions to follow for the proper drilling and turning sequence as well as for the size of blank you will need.

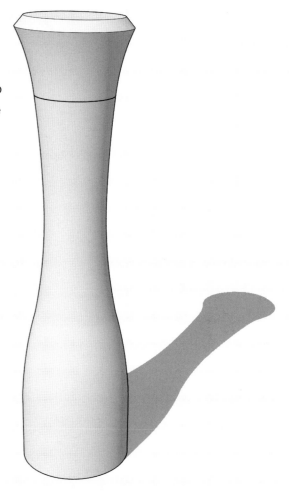

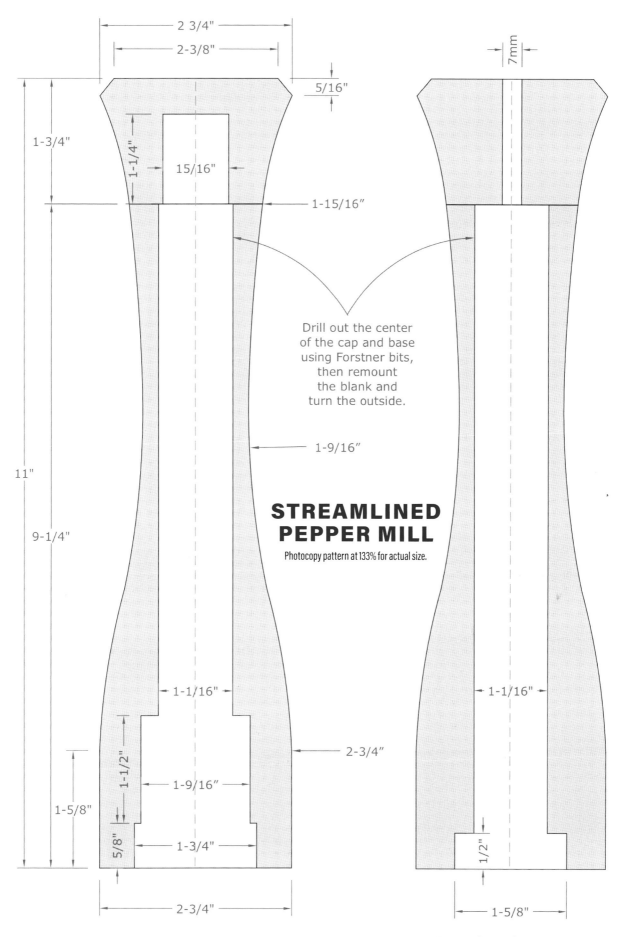

2 3/4"

2-3/8"

5/16"

1-3/4"

1-1/4"

15/16"

1-15/16"

7mm

Drill out the center
of the cap and base
using Forstner bits,
then remount
the blank and
turn the outside.

1-9/16"

11"

9-1/4"

STREAMLINED
PEPPER MILL

Photocopy pattern at 133% for actual size.

1-1/16"

1-1/16"

1-1/2"

1-9/16"

2-3/4"

1-5/8"

5/8"

1-3/4"

1/2"

2-3/4"

1-5/8"

For CrushGrind mechanism

For traditional mechanism

CLASSIC PEPPER MILL

A fairly simple version of the traditional pepper mill. The design offers you several opportunities for variation: You could change the simple curve on the base to a graceful S-curve. You could cut two beads on the base instead of one or omit the beads altogether. You could also make the spherical cap smaller or turn it with a compound curve, like the onion domes on some churches.

Pepper mill kits typically come with instructions to follow for the proper drilling and turning sequence as well as for the size of blank you will need. Some CrushGrind kits require a notch to be shaped in the base to hold locking tabs on the grinding mechanism.

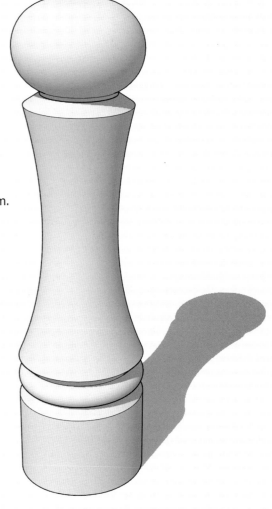

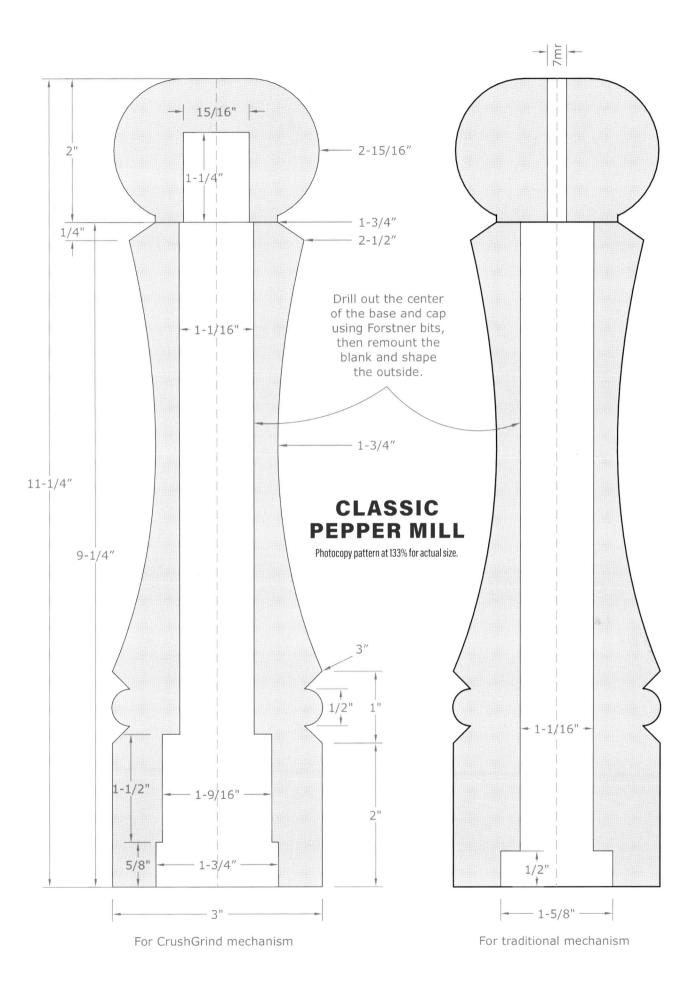

15/16"

2"

2-15/16"

1-1/4"

1/4"

1-3/4"

2-1/2"

7mr

Drill out the center
of the base and cap
using Forstner bits,
then remount the
blank and shape
the outside.

1-1/16"

1-3/4"

CLASSIC
PEPPER MILL

Photocopy pattern at 133% for actual size.

11-1/4"

9-1/4"

3"

1/2"   1"

1-1/16"

1-1/2"   1-9/16"

2"

5/8"   1-3/4"

1/2"

3"

1-5/8"

For CrushGrind mechanism

For traditional mechanism

MODERN PEPPER MILL

This piece should be very easy to turn, as it is a simple cylinder with a slightly crowned top. Three sets of grooves and some chamfers add visual interest. You can cut the grooves with a skew chisel or point tool. Or, if you turn the mill from a light wood, you can burn in the grooves with a length of wire pressed into the wood.

Like the other pepper mill patterns, this one is designed for either a CrushGrind or a traditional mechanism. Pepper mill kits typically come with instructions to follow for the proper drilling and turning sequence as well as for the size of blank you will need. Some CrushGrind kits require a notch to be shaped in the base to hold locking tabs on the grinding mechanism.

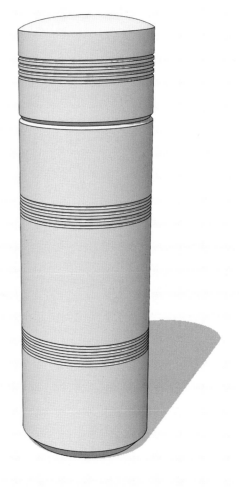

MODERN
PEPPER MILL

Photocopy pattern at 133% for actual size.

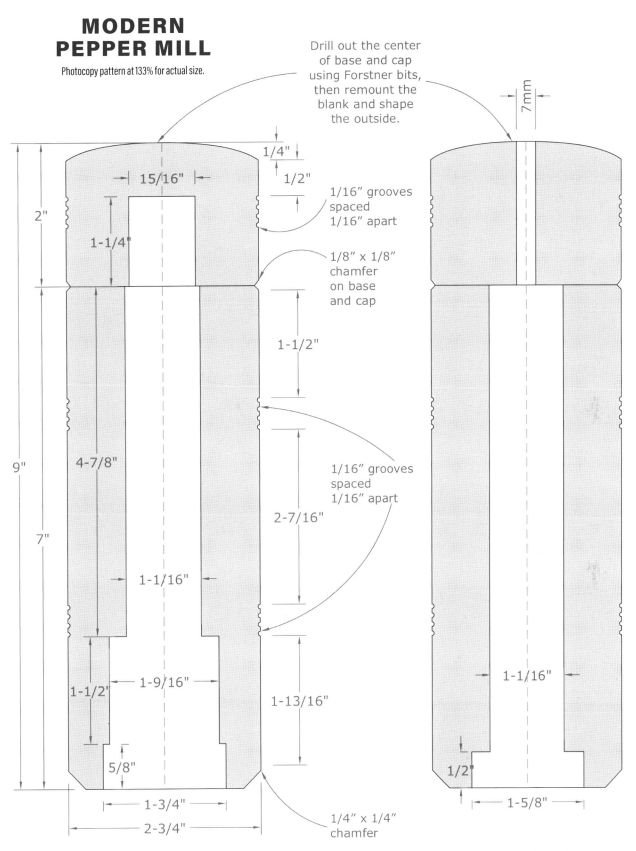

Drill out the center of base and cap using Forstner bits, then remount the blank and shape the outside.

1/4"

1/2"

15/16"

2"

1-1/4"

7mm

1/16" grooves spaced 1/16" apart

1/8" x 1/8" chamfer on base and cap

1-1/2"

9"

4-7/8"

7"

1/16" grooves spaced 1/16" apart

2-7/16"

1-1/16"

1-1/16"

1-9/16"

1-1/2"

1-13/16"

5/8"

1/2"

1-3/4"

2-3/4"

1/4" x 1/4" chamfer

1-5/8"

For CrushGrind mechanism

For traditional mechanism

TRADITIONAL PEPPER MILL

This variation on the traditional design offers a traditional S-curve, coupled with a pair of solid beads on the bottom. And there are ample opportunities for personalization. You could, for example, omit the small bead near the top or turn a cove there instead. You can also add or subtract large beads near the base.

Pepper mill kits typically come with instructions to follow for the proper drilling and turning sequence as well as for the size of blank you will need. Some CrushGrind kits require a notch to be shaped in the base to hold locking tabs on the grinding mechanism.

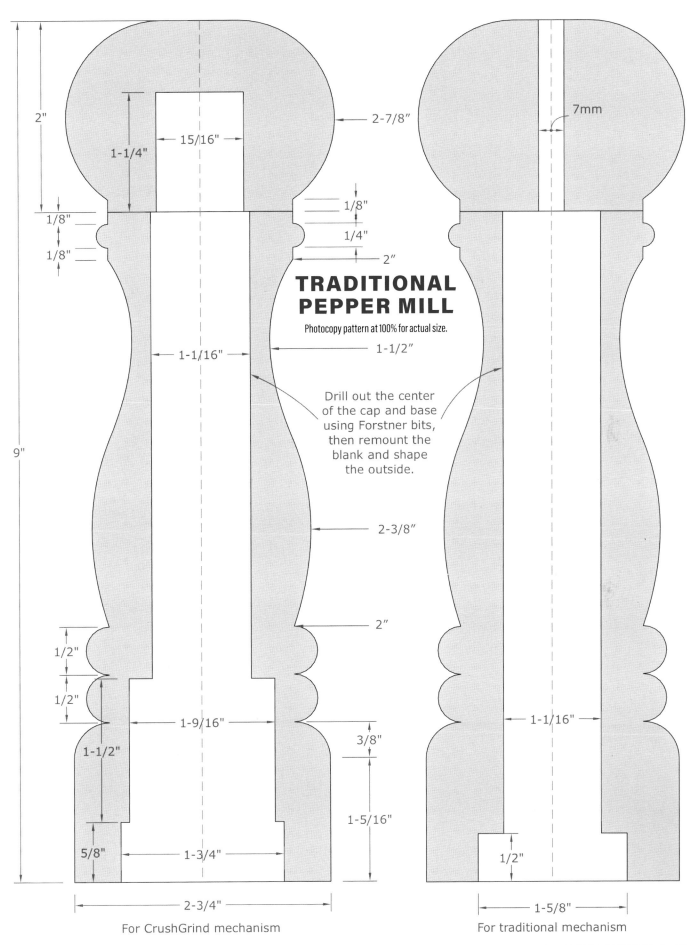

2"

2-7/8"

7mm

1-1/4"

15/16"

1/8"

1/8"

1/8"

1/4"

2"

TRADITIONAL
PEPPER MILL
Photocopy pattern at 100% for actual size.

1-1/16"

1-1/2"

Drill out the center
of the cap and base
using Forstner bits,
then remount the
blank and shape
the outside.

2-3/8"

9"

2"

1/2"

1/2"

1-9/16"

3/8"

1-1/16"

1-1/2"

1-5/16"

5/8"

1-3/4"

1/2"

2-3/4"

1-5/8"

For CrushGrind mechanism

For traditional mechanism

GEOMETRIC PEPPER MILL

What could be simpler than a cylinder and a sphere? This geometric duo looks right at home with modern décor. You could use this pattern to turn both a pepper mill and a salt mill. Choose a light wood like maple or birch for the salt mill; mahogany, rosewood, or black walnut for the pepper mill. You can also easily adapt the design for a taller set of mills.

Pepper mill kits typically come with instructions to follow for the proper drilling and turning sequence as well as for the size of blank you will need. Some CrushGrind kits require a notch to be shaped in the base to hold locking tabs on the grinding mechanism.

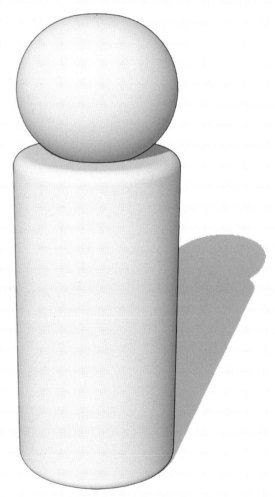

GEOMETRIC PEPPER MILL

Photocopy pattern at 100% for actual size.

Drill out the center of the cap and base using Forstner bits, then remount the blank and shape the outside.

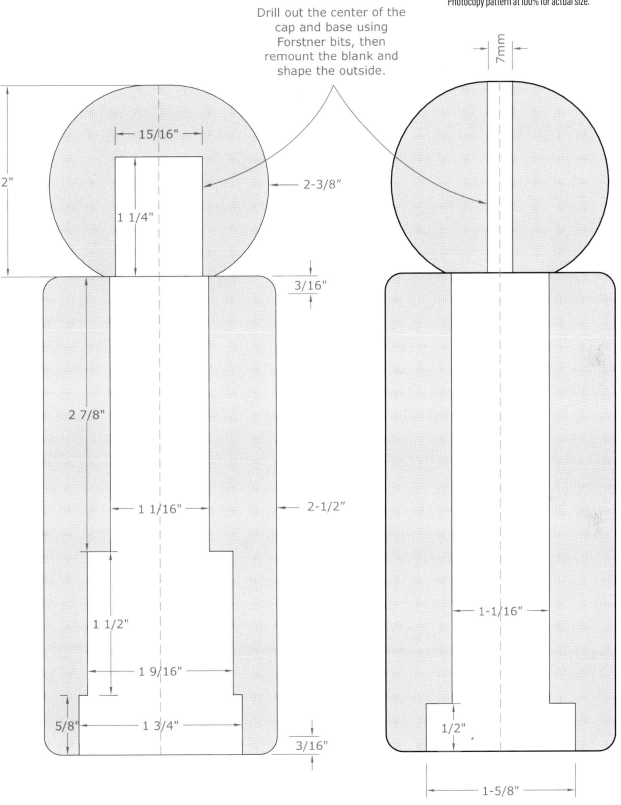

15/16"

2"

1 1/4"

2-3/8"

7mm

3/16"

2 7/8"

1 1/16"

2-1/2"

1 1/2"

1 9/16"

5/8"

1 3/4"

3/16"

1-1/16"

1/2"

1-5/8"

For CrushGrind mechanism

For traditional mechanism

MAÎTRE D'S PEPPER MILL

At more than a foot tall, this towering pepper mill is inspired by the ones used by waiters at high-end restaurants. Make your next dinner at home special by seasoning your loved one's meals with freshly ground pepper at the tableside. Like the other pepper mill patterns, this one is designed for either a CrushGrind or a traditional grinding mechanism.

Pepper mill kits typically come with instructions to follow for the proper drilling and turning sequence as well as for the size of blank you will need. Some CrushGrind kits require a notch to be shaped in the base to hold locking tabs on the grinding mechanism.

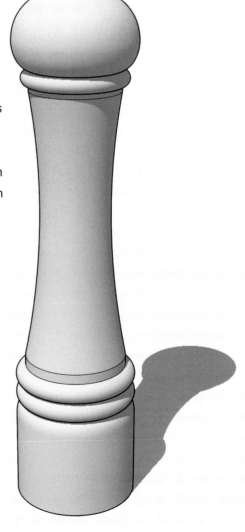

MAÎTRE D'S PEPPER MILL

Photocopy pattern at 133% for actual size.

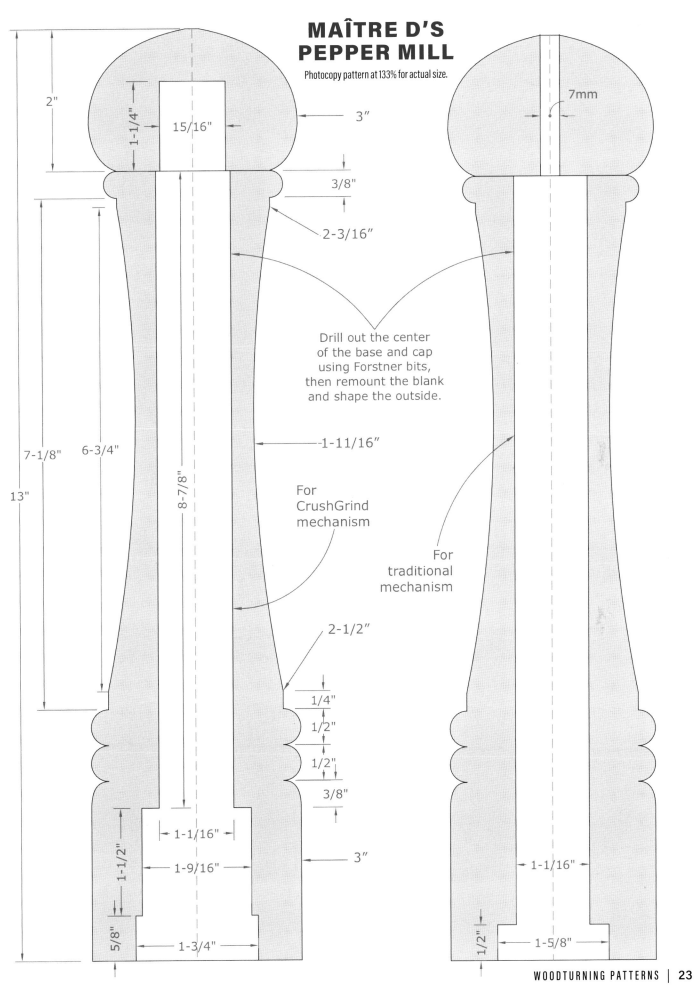

2"

1-1/4"

15/16"

3"

3/8"

2-3/16"

7mm

7-1/8"

6-3/4"

13"

8-7/8"

Drill out the center
of the base and cap
using Forstner bits,
then remount the blank
and shape the outside.

1-11/16"

For
CrushGrind
mechanism

For
traditional
mechanism

2-1/2"

1/4"

1/2"

1/2"

3/8"

1-1/16"

1-9/16"

1-1/2"

3"

5/8"

1-3/4"

1/2"

1-5/8"

1-1/16"

SALT & PEPPER CELLARS

Salt cellars, while somewhat unfamiliar now, were used during the Middle Ages and Renaissance at the tables of both rich and poor. They are ideal for larger grained salts and spices that clump or are unable to fit through the holes in a normal shaker. These matching salt and pepper cellars are essentially small turned boxes with tight-fitting lids. Each box is 3 in. high and 2 in. in diameter. The turning will go quickly if you do most of the hollowing with a Forstner bit.

To distinguish the salt from the pepper, turn one from a light-colored wood like maple; the other, from a darker wood like mahogany or black walnut. Or, turn both from a lighter wood, but burn lines in one by holding a piece of wire against the wood to identify the pepper cellar. For the salt cellar, cut small grooves with the point of a skew.

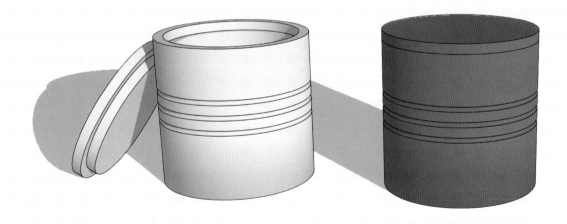

SALT & PEPPER
CELLARS

Photocopy pattern at 100% for actual size.

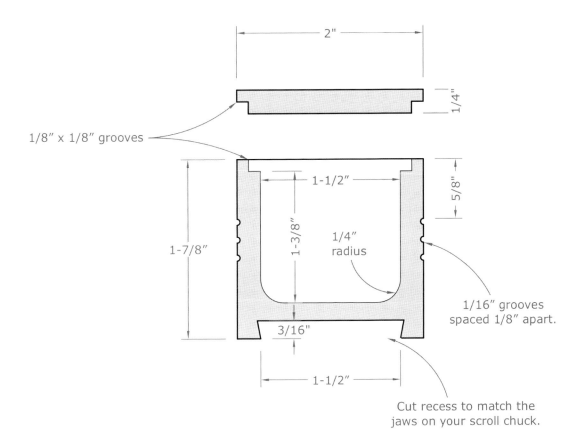

2"

1/4"

1/8" x 1/8" grooves

1-1/2"

5/8"

1-3/8"

1/4"
radius

1-7/8"

1/16" grooves
spaced 1/8" apart.

3/16"

1-1/2"

Cut recess to match the
jaws on your scroll chuck.

BOTTLE STOPPERS, PART ONE

Small stoppers like these are quick and easy to turn, and they give you an opportunity to use exotic woods with great grain and figure. Turning a set of unique shapes makes it easy to tell the white wine from the red or the gin from the vermouth. With the stopper shape on the left, you can make each one in a set unique by gluing different glass or metal inserts in the top recess.

The turning is glued onto a shaft with an attached stopper, either a cork or a tapered, flexible plastic piece. Be sure to match the hole in the base of the stopper to the size of the shaft in the kit you buy.

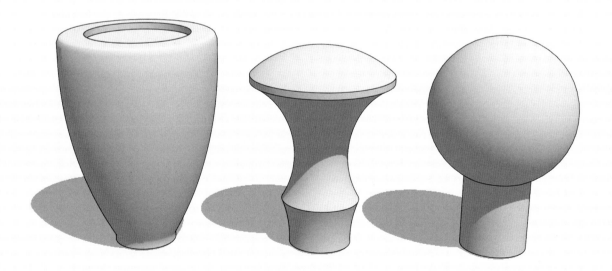

BOTTLE STOPPERS,
PART ONE

Photocopy pattern at 100% for actual size.

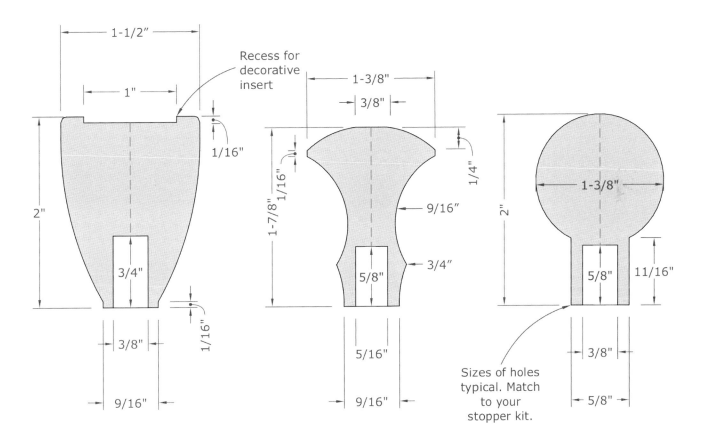

1-1/2"

1"

Recess for decorative insert

1/16"

2"

3/4"

3/8"

1/16"

9/16"

1-3/8"

3/8"

1/16"

1/4"

1-7/8"

9/16"

5/8"

3/4"

5/16"

9/16"

2"

1-3/8"

5/8"

11/16"

Sizes of holes typical. Match to your stopper kit.

3/8"

5/8"

BOTTLE STOPPERS, PART TWO

These stoppers are a bit more creative than the last set—adding multiple grooves and beads can make it easier to remove the stopper from a bottle when it has been wedged in tightly. One is adorned with two sets of beads. One is all angles and V-grooves. And one tapers gracefully from top to base.

The turning is glued onto a shaft with an attached stopper, either a cork or a tapered, flexible plastic piece. Be sure to match the hole in the base of the stopper to the size of the shaft in the kit you buy.

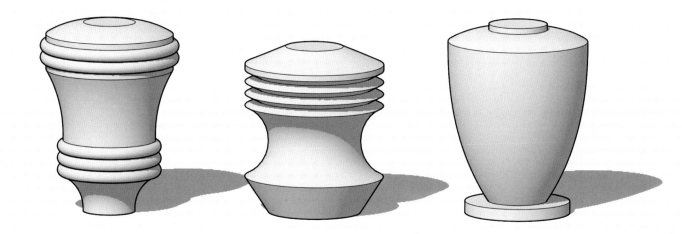

BOTTLE STOPPERS, PART TWO

Photocopy pattern at 100% for actual size.

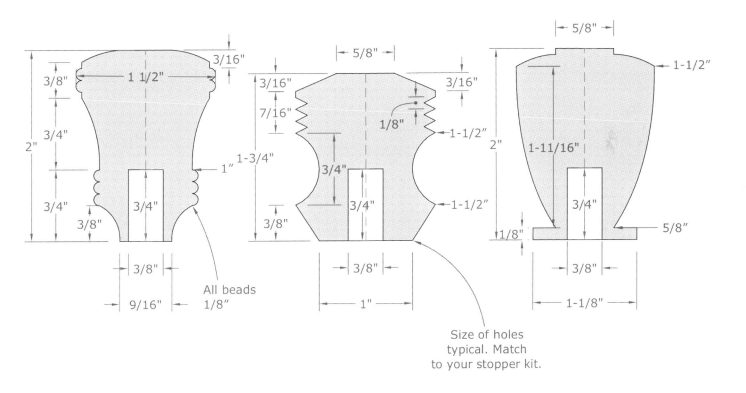

All beads 1/8"

Size of holes typical. Match to your stopper kit.

BOTTLE STOPPERS, PART THREE

This elegant trio features an egg-shaped piece with simple grooves, a more traditional globe and peg, and a curved and coved design reminiscent of a chess piece.

In each case, the turning is glued onto a shaft with an attached stopper, either a cork or a tapered, flexible plastic piece. Be sure to match the hole in the base of the stopper to the size of the shaft in the kit you buy.

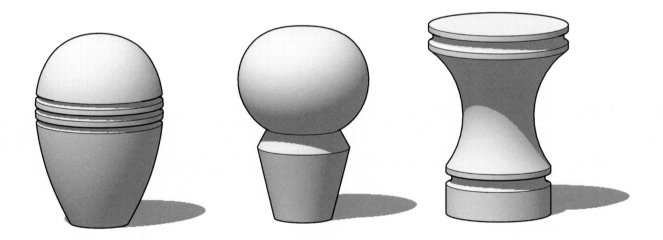

BOTTLE STOPPERS,
PART THREE

Photocopy pattern at 100% for actual size.

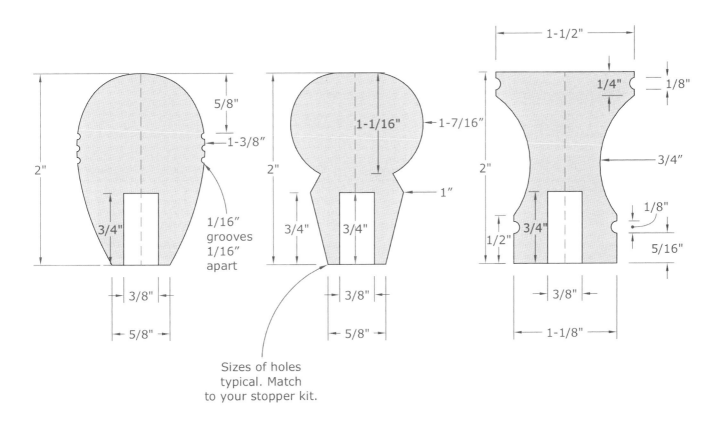

5/8"
1-3/8"
2"
3/4"
1/16" grooves 1/16" apart
3/8"
5/8"

1-1/16"
1-7/16"
2"
3/4"
1"
3/4"
3/8"
5/8"

Sizes of holes typical. Match to your stopper kit.

1-1/2"
1/4"
1/8"
1-7/16"
3/4"
2"
1/8"
3/4"
5/16"
1/2"
3/8"
1-1/8"

Kitchenware

ALL-PURPOSE SCOOP

Every kitchen needs scoops for flour, sugar, coffee, tea, spices, and various other dry goods. Richard Raffan, one of the world's leading woodturners, made and sold thousands of scoops like this one when he took up turning as a livelihood.

The pattern shows a wall of 1/16 in. for the scoop, but there's no magic in that number. Turn it as thin as you can, and try to create a wall that is consistent in thickness.

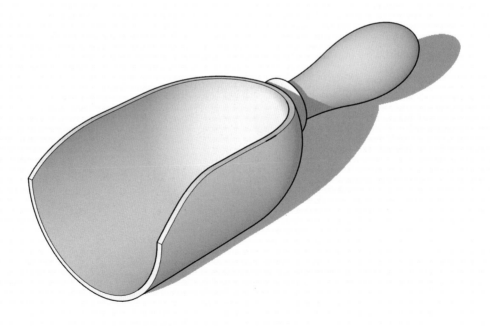

ALL-PURPOSE
SCOOP

Photocopy pattern at 100% for actual size.

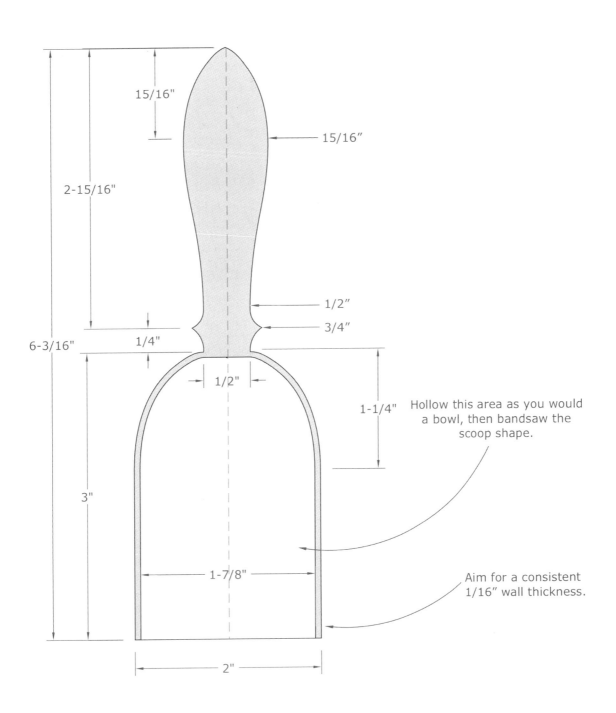

15/16"

15/16"

2-15/16"

1/2"

3/4"

1/4"

6-3/16"

1/2"

1-1/4"

Hollow this area as you would a bowl, then bandsaw the scoop shape.

3"

1-7/8"

Aim for a consistent 1/16" wall thickness.

2"

COFFEE SCOOP

Mike Peace, a prolific woodturner in Georgia, showed how to turn this uniquely shaped scoop in an article in *American Woodturner,* the journal of the American Association of Woodturners. Begin the turning with the work held between centers. Then turn the handle and shape the sphere for the outside of the bowl.

Finishing the scoop requires mounting the work in a donut chuck, a shop-made fixture consisting of two donut shaped pieces of wood that bolt together. You hold the piece securely in the donut chuck while you hollow the bowl.

The dimensions shown for the bowl are ideal for a single scoop of coffee.

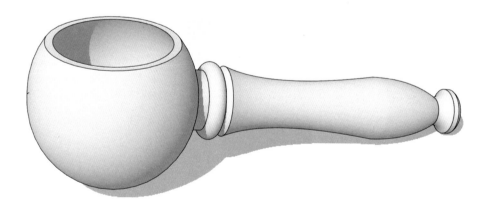

COFFEE SCOOP

Photocopy pattern at 100% for actual size.

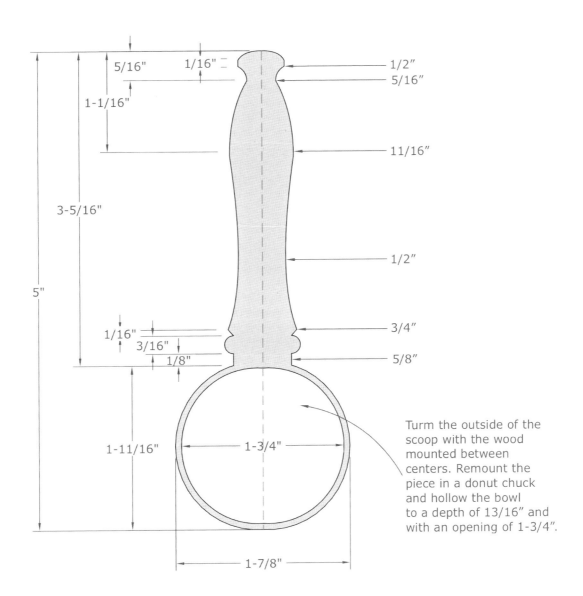

5/16"

1/16"

1-1/16"

3-5/16"

5"

1/16"

3/16"

1/8"

1-11/16"

1/2"

5/16"

11/16"

1/2"

3/4"

5/8"

1-3/4"

1-7/8"

Turm the outside of the scoop with the wood mounted between centers. Remount the piece in a donut chuck and hollow the bowl to a depth of 13/16" and with an opening of 1-3/4".

Kitchenware

HONEY DIPPER

A classic project for beginning turners, the honey dipper is quick and easy to make. It's also a handy and stylish serving utensil. When turning, it's best to turn the grooved knob at the tailstock end, then work back toward the headstock as you shape the handle. Do most of the sanding at the lathe, and hand-sand the ends once you have parted off the dipper.

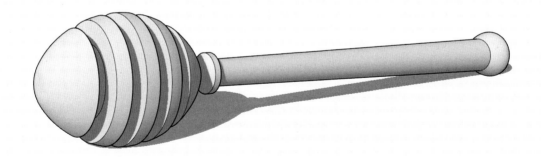

HONEY
DIPPER

Photocopy pattern at 100% for actual size.

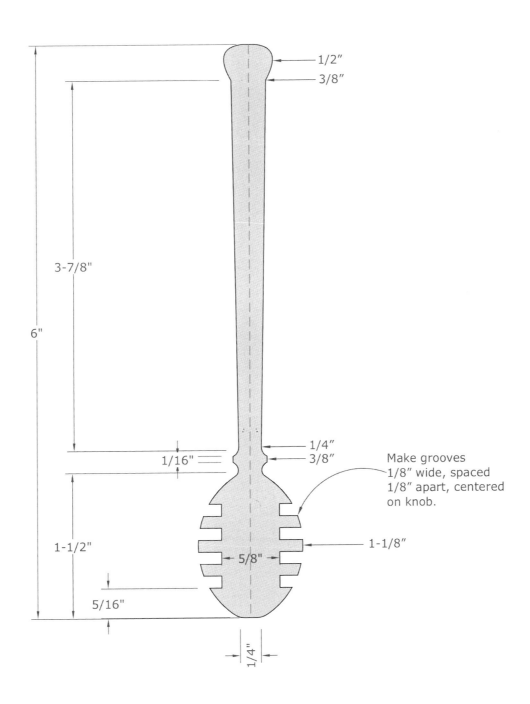

1/2"

3/8"

3-7/8"

6"

1/16"

1/4"

3/8"

Make grooves
1/8" wide, spaced
1/8" apart, centered
on knob.

1-1/2"

5/8"

1-1/8"

5/16"

1/4"

Kitchenware

CUSTOM CHOPSTICKS

Looks can be deceiving. You might think it's easy to turn a pair of chopsticks. In truth, turning something long and thin can be a challenge. It's also a great way to hone your turning skills.

For the 9 in. chopsticks shown here, begin with a blank that's 5/16 in. square and 10 in. long. Use a Jacobs chuck, a collet chuck, or a scroll chuck with pin jaws in the headstock to hold one end; support the other end with a cup center in the tailstock. Work from the tailstock toward the headstock, turning the round, tapered portion of the chopstick. Take light cuts with a sharp tool, and gently support the wood with your free hand to keep it from flexing.

Use sandpaper or take light cuts with a turning tool to ease the corners of the square ends of the chopsticks. Part off the piece at the headstock end and sand both ends smooth.

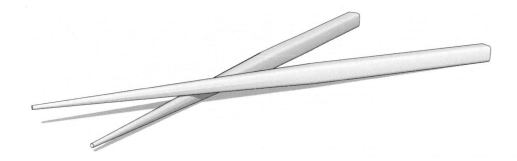

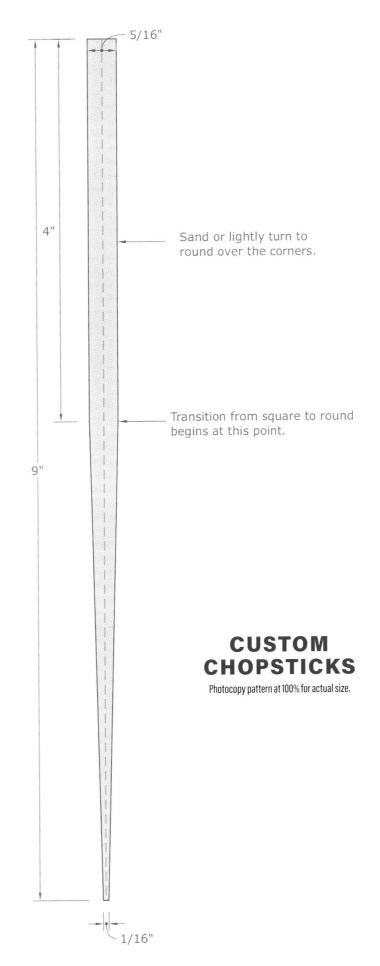

5/16"

4"

Sand or lightly turn to
round over the corners.

Transition from square to round
begins at this point.

9"

CUSTOM
CHOPSTICKS

Photocopy pattern at 100% for actual size.

1/16"

GADGET HANDLES, PART ONE

Nothing lets you know you're in a maker's kitchen like handmade handles on kitchen utensils. These handles will fit kits for pizza cutters, cheese slicers, bottle openers, ice-cream scoops, and more. Almost all implements have a post that fits into a hole in the handle. But kits aren't uniform from brand to brand, so adjust the size of the hole and the base to fit the kit you buy.

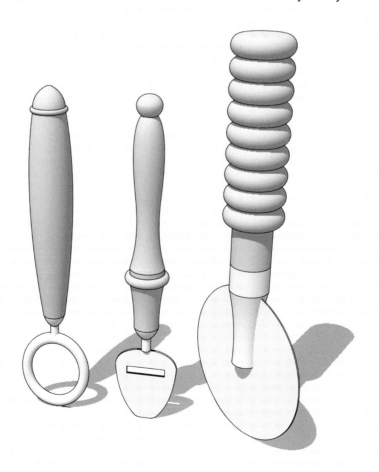

GADGET HANDLES,
PART ONE

Photocopy pattern at 100% for actual size.

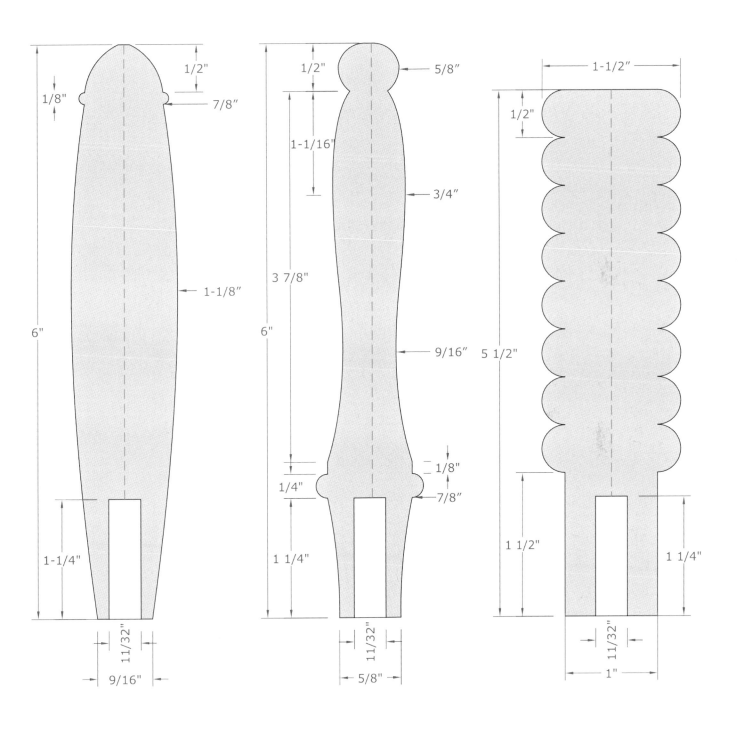

GADGET HANDLES, PART TWO

Here are three more shapes that will work well with a range of kitchen utensils, including a pizza cutter, salad servers, a cheese slicer, or a peeler. The basic dimensions shown here are also a great jumping-off point for creating a design of your own.

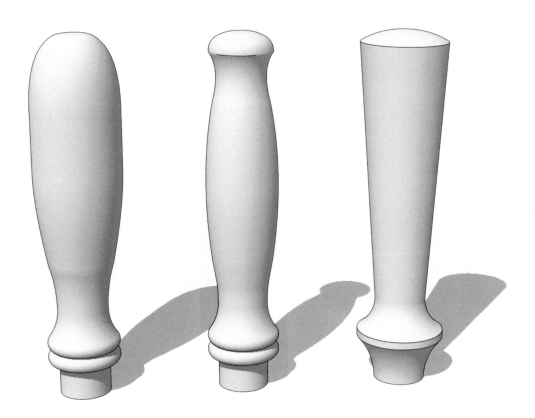

GADGET HANDLES, PART TWO

Photocopy pattern at 100% for actual size.

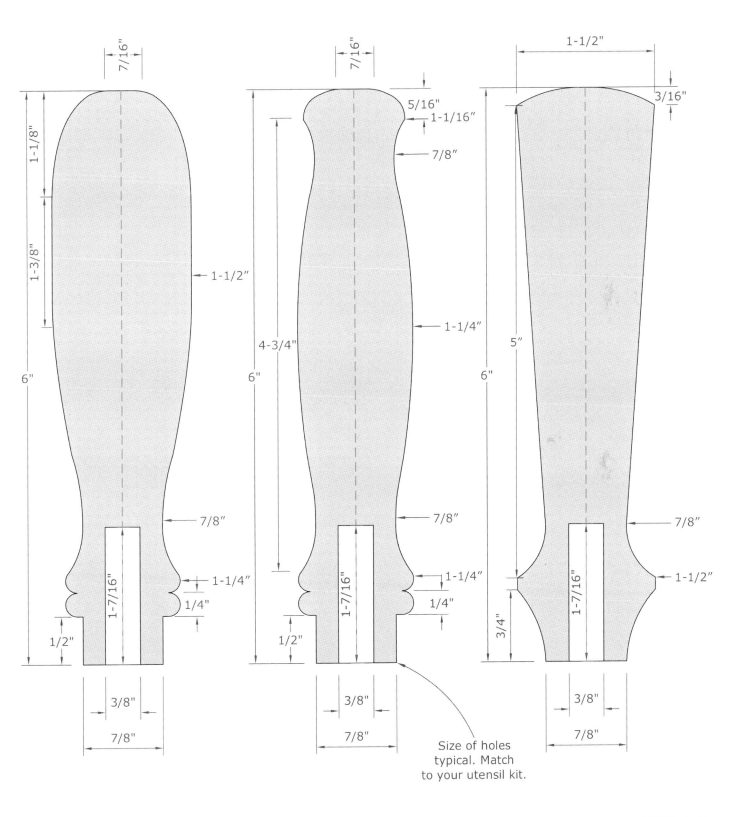

7/16"

1-1/8"

1-3/8"

6"

1-1/2"

7/8"

1-7/16"

1-1/4"

1/4"

1/2"

3/8"

7/8"

7/16"

5/16"

1-1/16"

7/8"

4-3/4"

6"

1-1/4"

7/8"

1-7/16"

1-1/4"

1/4"

1/2"

3/8"

7/8"

Size of holes typical. Match to your utensil kit.

1-1/2"

3/16"

5"

6"

7/8"

1-1/2"

3/4"

1-7/16"

3/8"

7/8"

GADGET HANDLES, PART THREE

Here are three more handles to choose from, ranging from a handle with plain, smooth curves to fancier curves embellished with large beads. As you turn these (or any handle pattern), stop the lathe periodically and hold the handle in progress to be sure it's comfortable in your hands. And remember that it's your turning, so feel free to adjust the shape as needed.

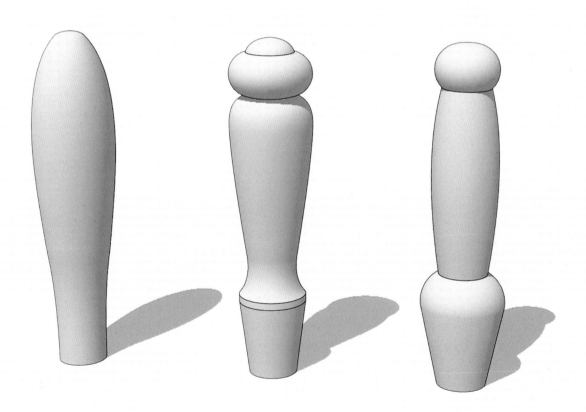

GADGET HANDLES, PART THREE

Photocopy pattern at 100% for actual size.

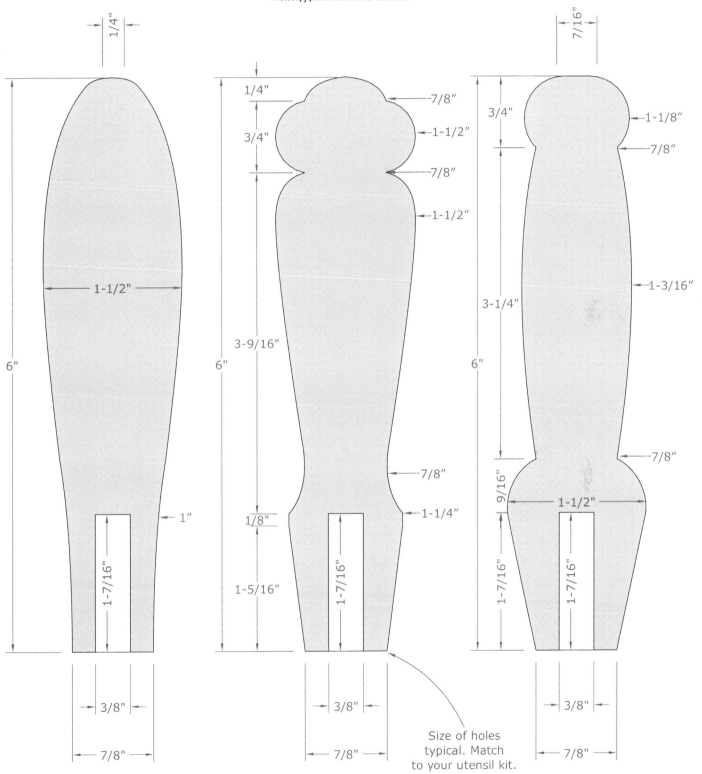

Size of holes typical. Match to your utensil kit.

FRENCH ROLLING PIN

A custom-turned rolling pin gets certain love in a baker's kitchen. You can also turn this classic piece of kitchenware quickly and easily. It's simply a long cylinder with gently tapered ends. The pattern shown here is for a 20-in. long rolling pin, but it can range in length anywhere from 18 to 22 in. When choosing stock, look for a durable tight-grained species like hard maple, quilted maple, or black walnut.

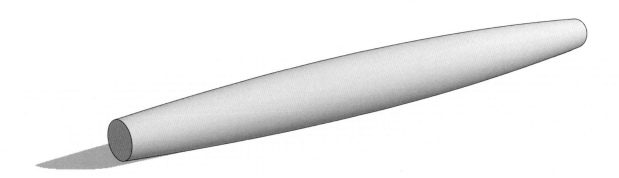

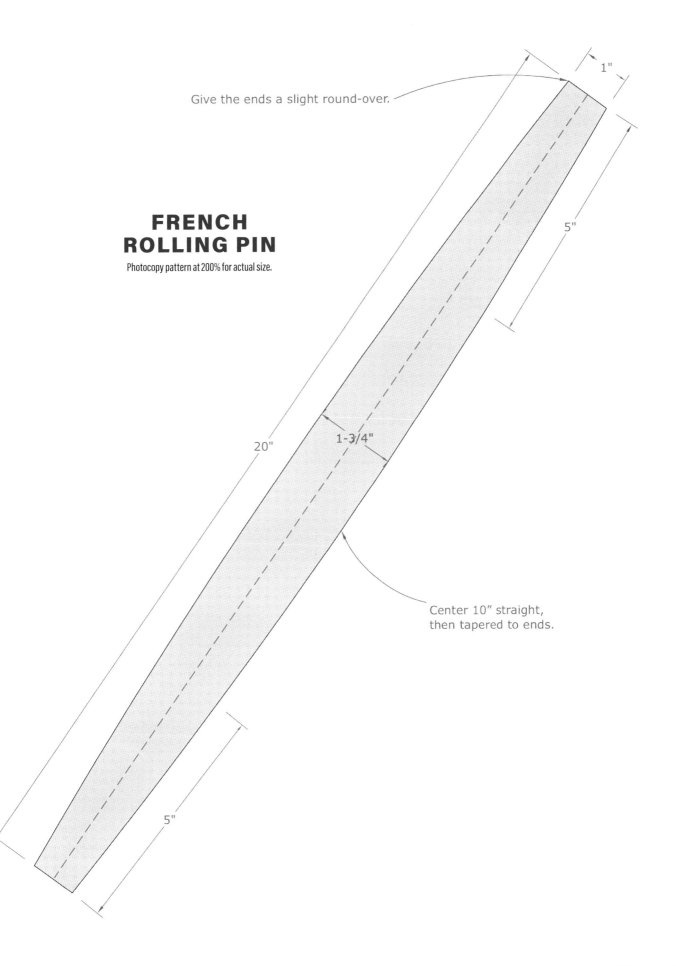

FRENCH ROLLING PIN

Photocopy pattern at 200% for actual size.

Give the ends a slight round-over.

1"

5"

20"

1-3/4"

Center 10" straight, then tapered to ends.

5"

LARGE BASTING BRUSH

The bristles for basting brushes come ready-made as a plug that is glued into a recess turned on the business end of the handle. The pattern shown here is for a set of bristles that measure 3/4-in. in diameter, a versatile all-around size. For specialty uses, smaller bristle sets are also available.

Because a basting brush is used around all sorts of liquids, it's a good idea to use a waterproof epoxy to attach the bristles.

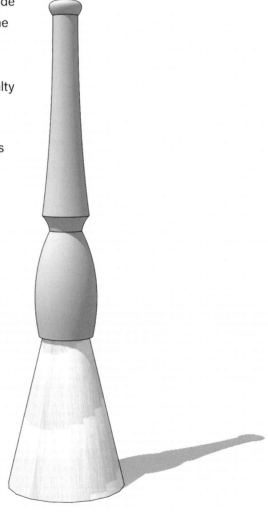

LARGE
BASTING BRUSH

Photocopy pattern at 100% for actual size.

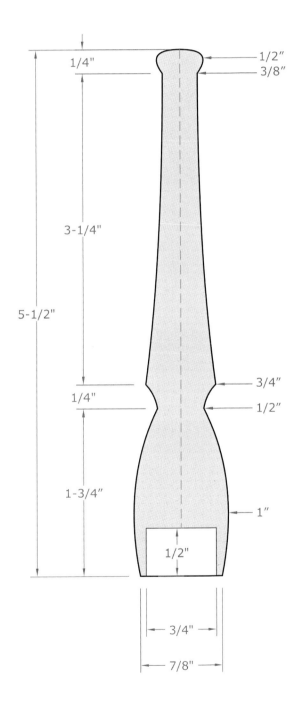

1/4"

1/2"
3/8"

3-1/4"

5-1/2"

3/4"

1/4"
1/2"

1-3/4"

1"

1/2"

3/4"

7/8"

TWO
BEER-TAP HANDLES

Making your own tap handles is much like making the all-purpose gadget handles shown on pages 40 to 45. The only real difference is that you use a special hanger bolt to screw the tap handle onto the metal faucet itself. Modify the pattern as needed so that the hole and base of the handle fit the kit you buy.

Many beer-tap suppliers offer a variety of finials for handles like these. The patterns have plenty of room at the top for you to add a finial if you wish.

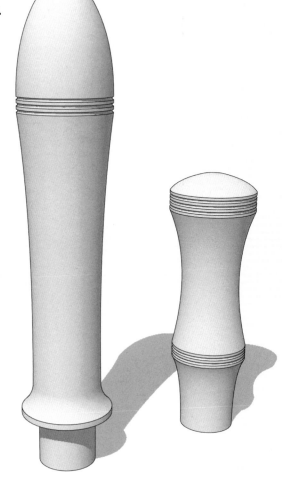

TWO
BEER-TAP HANDLES

Photocopy pattern at 100% for actual size.

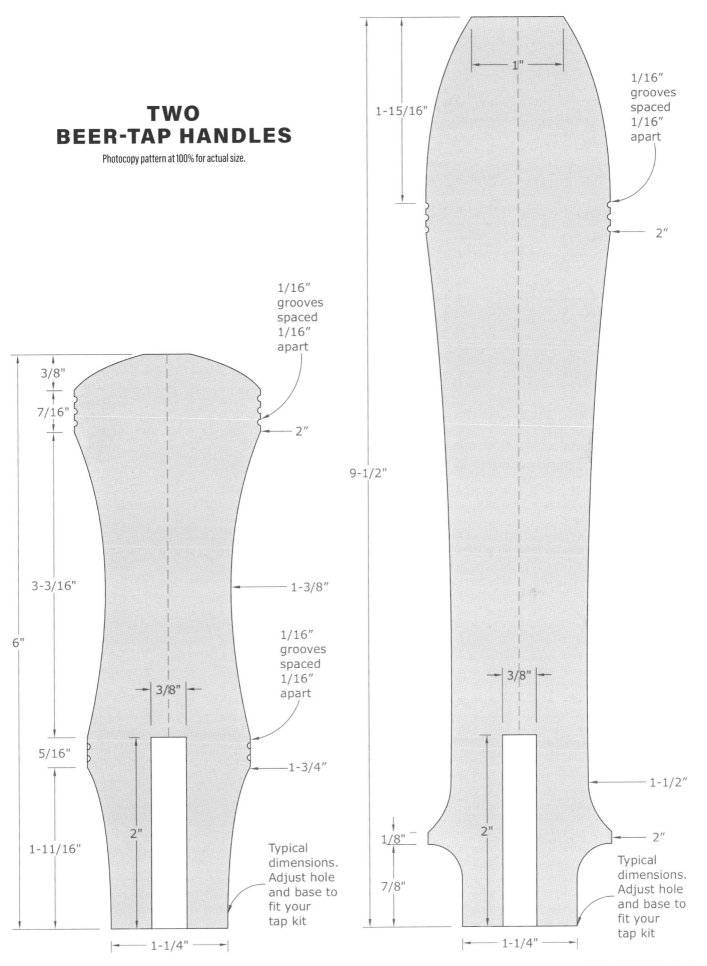

1/16"
grooves
spaced
1/16"
apart

3/8"

7/16"

2"

6"

3-3/16"

1-3/8"

1/16"
grooves
spaced
1/16"
apart

3/8"

5/16"

1-3/4"

2"

1-11/16"

Typical
dimensions.
Adjust hole
and base to
fit your
tap kit

1-1/4"

1"

1-15/16"

1/16"
grooves
spaced
1/16"
apart

2"

9-1/2"

3/8"

1-1/2"

2"

1/8"

7/8"

2"

Typical
dimensions.
Adjust hole
and base to
fit your
tap kit

1-1/4"

PATTERNS

Playthings & Ornaments

Woodturning doesn't have to be all business or time-consuming. Turning a small spin top takes only a couple of minutes, but you can watch a child enjoy the toy for hours.

Turning a croquet mallet can be a quick project or the start of a complete croquet set. You can even turn the balls, either working freehand at the lathe or with the aid of a sphere-cutting jig.

And, at holiday time, there is no better way to showcase your turning than by making one-of-a-kind ornaments for your own tree or to give as gifts.

A QUARTET OF SPIN TOPS

Making tops is a good way to use up small scraps of wood and please kids in the process. Tops are also good projects for refining your spindle-turning skills. Many woodturning clubs make dozens—sometimes hundreds—of tops at craft-fair demonstrations or to donate to children's hospitals and charitable organizations.

The four patterns shown here should be enough to whet your appetite. In truth, you can make tops with an infinite variety of beads, grooves, and other embellishments, and decorate them with ink, paint, or permanent markers.

The best tops should spin for about a minute, and spin so smoothly that they don't seem to be moving at all. (This is called sleeping.) The secret is to make the top with a low center of gravity and a thin stem.

A QUARTET
OF SPIN TOPS

Photocopy pattern at 100% for actual size.

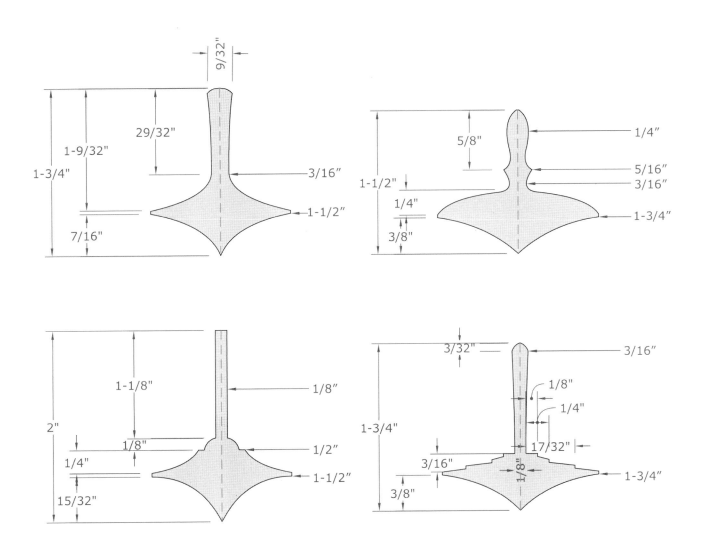

BASEBALL BAT

The best woods for baseball bats are ash, maple, and hickory. Look for a blank with the clearest, straightest grain you can find. It's one thing for a big-league player to hit a broken-bat single, but it's the last thing you want when you're swinging the bat you made yourself.

Current Major League Baseball regulations specify that a bat must be 2.61 in. thick at the barrel and no more than 42 in. long. Bats typically range in length from 31 to 34 in. To determine the best size for you, extend one arm straight out to the side; measure the distance from the center of your chest to the tip of your index finger.

You can use most of the same dimensions shown here if you want to turn a softball bat. Just adjust the barrel to 2-1/4 in. in diameter.

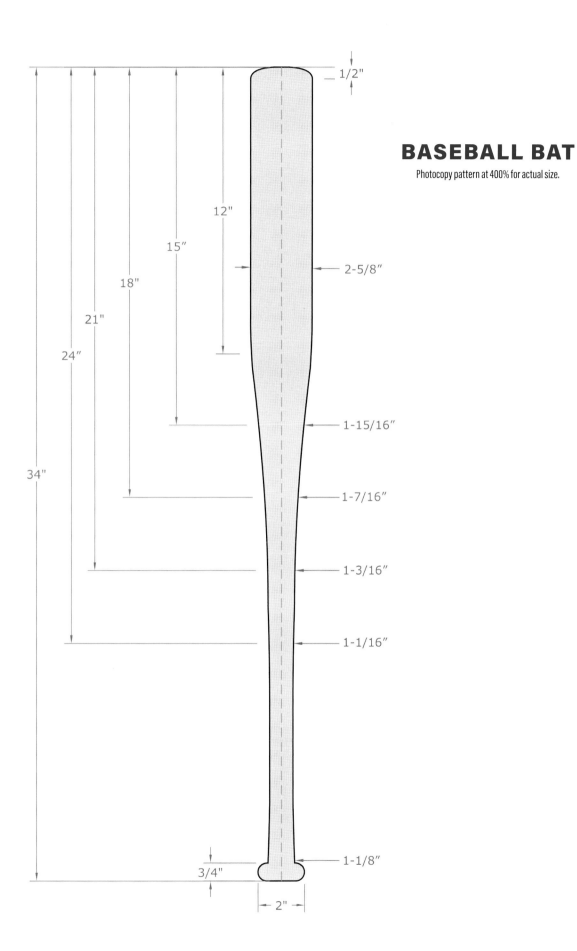

BASEBALL BAT

Photocopy pattern at 400% for actual size.

1/2"

12"

15"

18"

21"

24"

34"

2-5/8"

1-15/16"

1-7/16"

1-3/16"

1-1/16"

1-1/8"

3/4"

2"

CROQUET MALLET

According to Britain's Croquet Association, few rules govern the size of a croquet mallet. But the association does offer a few guidelines: The typical head is 9 to 9-1/2 in. long, but the pros can play with a mallet head that's as much as 12 in. long. As for the length of the handle, hang your arm at your side and measure the distance from your wrist to the ground, then add an inch to that measurement.

High-end croquet mallets have metal hoops on the ends of the head to prevent it from mushrooming. On the pattern shown here, the chamfer on the ends serves the same purpose.

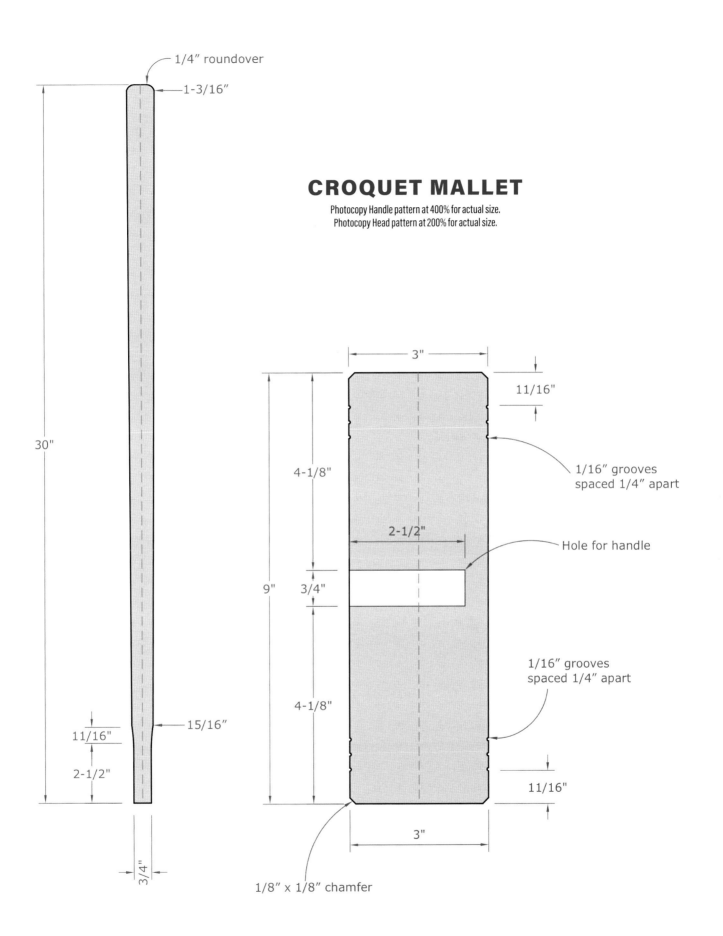

CROQUET MALLET

Photocopy Handle pattern at 400% for actual size.
Photocopy Head pattern at 200% for actual size.

1/4" roundover

1-3/16"

30"

15/16"

11/16"

2-1/2"

3/4"

3"

11/16"

4-1/8"

2-1/2"

1/16" grooves
spaced 1/4" apart

Hole for handle

9"

3/4"

4-1/8"

1/16" grooves
spaced 1/4" apart

11/16"

3"

1/8" x 1/8" chamfer

BABY RATTLE

Baby rattles are one of those projects that make people scratch their heads and ask, "How did you do that?" If you do it right, people won't be able to figure out how you got a noisemaker inside what appears to be a solid piece of wood. But renowned turner Richard Raffan—among others—has passed along the secret.

Begin by splitting your turning blank in half, then hollow out a portion of each half to create the inside of the rattle head. Put in something to make the noise, such as a nut or a couple of washers, and glue the two halves together. Once the glue cures, chuck the piece up and turn the outside of the rattle.

You can leave the piece unfinished. But if you want to apply a finish, use something food-safe, such as mineral oil.

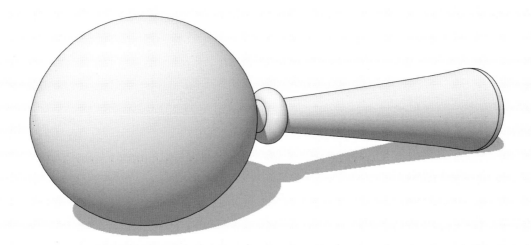

BABY RATTLE

Photocopy pattern at 100% for actual size.

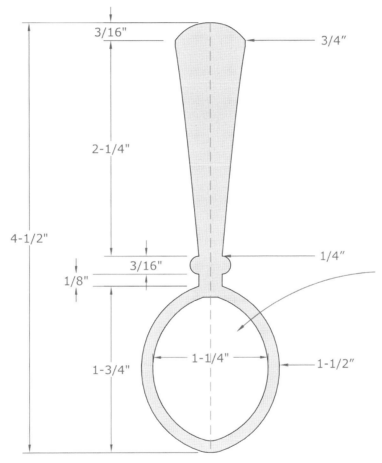

3/16"

3/4″

2-1/4"

4-1/2"

3/16"

1/8"

1/4″

Split workpiece in half. Hollow the head on each half. Insert a noisemaker and glue the halves together. Finish by turning the handle.

1-3/4"

1-1/4"

1-1/2″

SEA URCHIN TREE ORNAMENT

The lumpy, bumpy surface of a sea urchin makes a striking focal point for a holiday tree ornament. Turned finials glued to the top and bottom of the urchin complete the piece.

Begin this piece by making the openings in the urchin as round as you can, so that the finials will fit tightly. Turn the finials to fit the urchin. Accordingly, most of the dimensions given with the pattern are there as a guide. Also, don't feel obliged to follow the shape of the finials shown on the pattern; make them as intricate as you like. Just be sure to work from the tailstock toward the headstock to prevent the workpiece from flexing or snapping as you turn.

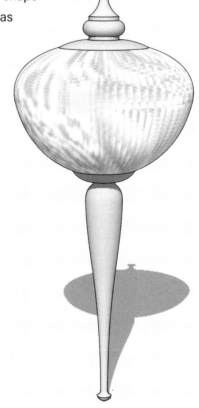

Some people leave the sea urchin in its natural color, but you can paint it or gild it with metallic mica powder, available from gilding suppliers on the Internet.

SEA URCHIN
TREE ORNAMENT

Photocopy pattern at 100% for actual size.

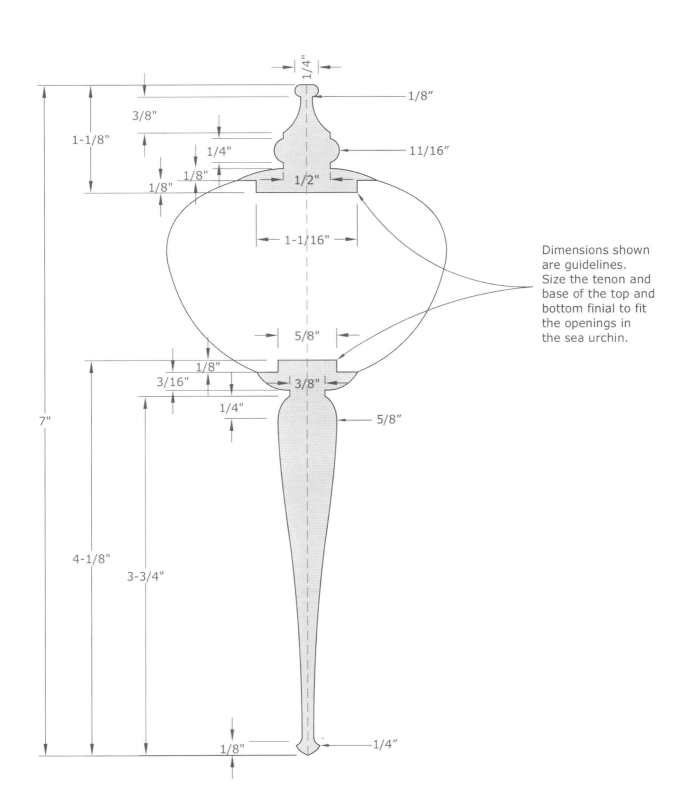

Dimensions shown
are guidelines.
Size the tenon and
base of the top and
bottom finial to fit
the openings in
the sea urchin.

MULTICOLORED TREE ORNAMENTS

The only difference between a multicolored ornament and any other is the blank you start with. For multicolored ornaments, glue up a blank from pieces of different woods ranging in thickness from 1/4 in. to 1/2 in. You can use strips the same thickness, or vary the thicknesses to create a pleasing pattern either vertically or horizontally. Or, you could turn these ornaments from Spectraply, a specialty plywood that comes in numerous color combinations.

Let the wood colors carry the day; keep the shape of the ornament reasonably simple. Once you've completed the turning, give it a glossy clear finish with lacquer or polyurethane.

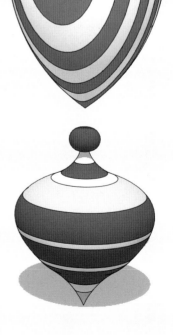

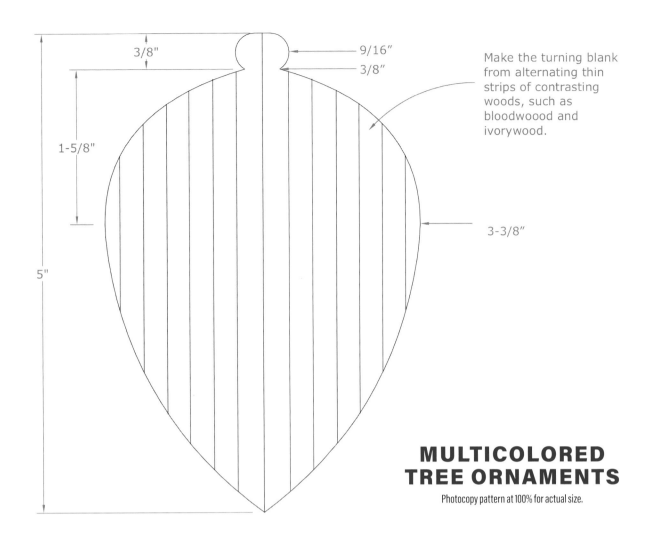

3/8"

9/16"

3/8"

Make the turning blank from alternating thin strips of contrasting woods, such as bloodwoood and ivorywood.

1-5/8"

3-3/8"

5"

MULTICOLORED TREE ORNAMENTS

Photocopy pattern at 100% for actual size.

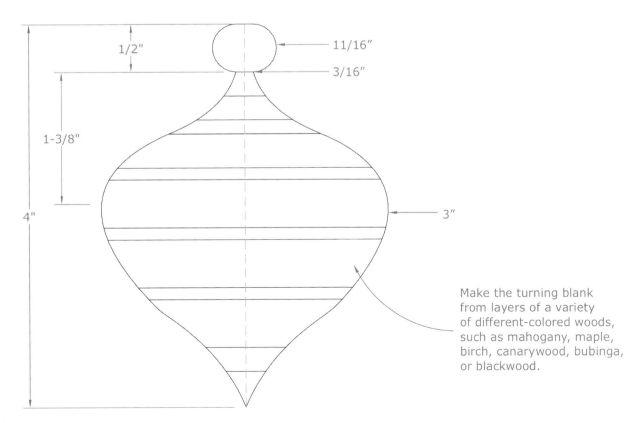

1/2"

11/16"

3/16"

1-3/8"

3"

4"

Make the turning blank from layers of a variety of different-colored woods, such as mahogany, maple, birch, canarywood, bubinga, or blackwood.

PATTERNS

CHAPTER

3

Knobs
& Finials

Small details can make or break the design for a piece of furniture. A well-chosen knob for a door or drawer, for example, can elevate the piece from nice to superb.

In this chapter, you'll find patterns for authentic Shaker knobs as well as patterns for several traditional styles. I've also included finials that will complement small turned boxes as well as period furniture.

SHAKER KNOBS & SHAKER PEG

Every turner should have an arsenal of knob designs to use, and these three classic Shaker designs are hard to beat. With either the knobs or the peg, you can easily scale them up if you need something larger. Authentic Shaker pegs come in a variety of lengths.

To turn these pieces, begin with the wood mounted between centers. Turn it round and shape the tenon. Then remount the piece, using either a Jacobs chuck, a collet chuck, or a scroll chuck with pin jaws to grip the tenon. If you need multiple identical knobs or pegs, paste a copy of the pattern onto cardboard or 1/8-in. plywood and cut out the outline of the shape to use as a gauge.

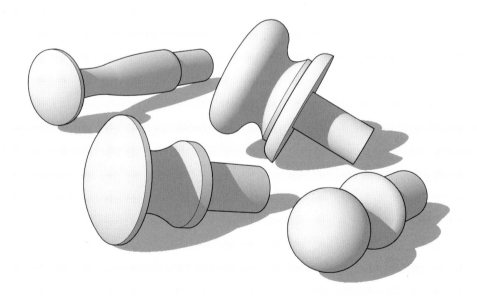

SHAKER KNOBS
& SHAKER PEG

Photocopy pattern at 100% for actual size.

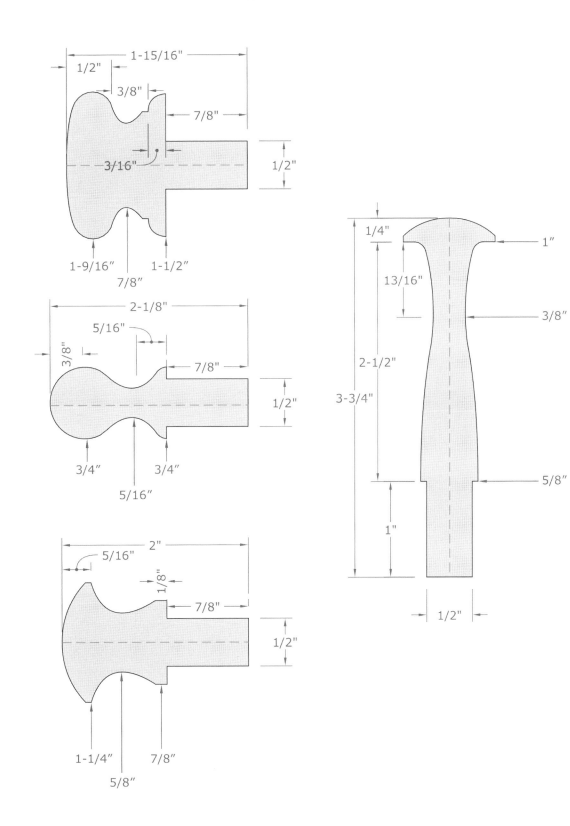

SEMICIRCULAR PULL

This pull was originally designed for drawers in a small Japanese-style case. The pattern can be scaled up for larger drawers or doors. The pull looks best when made from a dark, figured wood such as rosewood or bubinga.

You can easily make identical multiples of the pull. Here's how: Cut rough blanks for as many pulls as you need; make them slightly larger than 2 in. square. Drill a 1-in. diameter hole in the center of each blank. Turn a mandrel—a 1-in.-diameter shaft that will hold the blanks on the lathe. Leave a shoulder on the headstock end of the mandrel, giving the blanks something to rest against. Slide the blanks onto the mandrel and saw it flush with the last blank. Put a piece of scrap against the last blank and bring the tailstock up to press against the scrap. Turn all the blanks to size, then turn lengths of 5/16-in. dowel for the posts. Saw each doughnut-shaped piece in half and drill a shallow hole in each for the post. Cut the posts to length and glue them into the holes. Drill a 5/16 in. diameter hole 1/4 in. deep in the drawer or door to accept the pull.

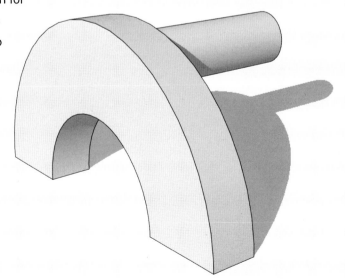

SEMICIRCULAR PULL

Photocopy pattern at 100% for actual size.

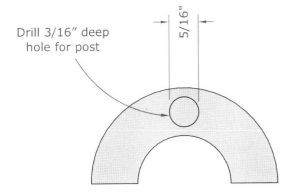

Drill 3/16" deep hole for post

5/16"

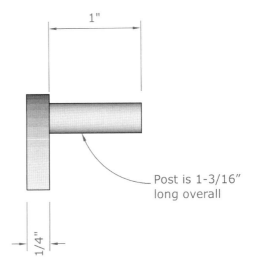

1"

1/4"

Post is 1-3/16" long overall

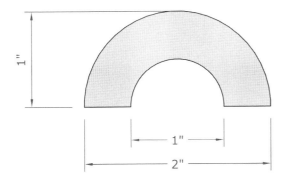

1"

1"

2"

A TRIO OF TRADITIONAL KNOBS

These three patterns are based on their brass and pewter counterparts, and all can work well on period furniture. The "beehive" pull—the one with grooves around its midsection—could also work well with Art Deco pieces. Like most knob patterns, these can easily be scaled up or down as needed.

To turn these knobs, make a screw chuck. Turn a tenon on a scrap block, so it will fit in a scroll chuck. Grab the block in the chuck and drill a pilot hole for a longer version of the screw you will use to attach the knob. Then drill a pilot hole in the turning blank for the knob and thread the blank onto your shopmade screw chuck. Turn the knob, unthread it, and you're done.

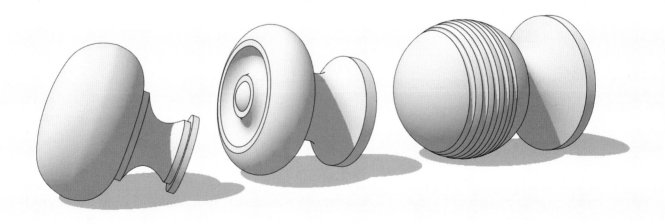

A TRIO OF
TRADITIONAL KNOBS

Photocopy pattern at 100% for actual size.

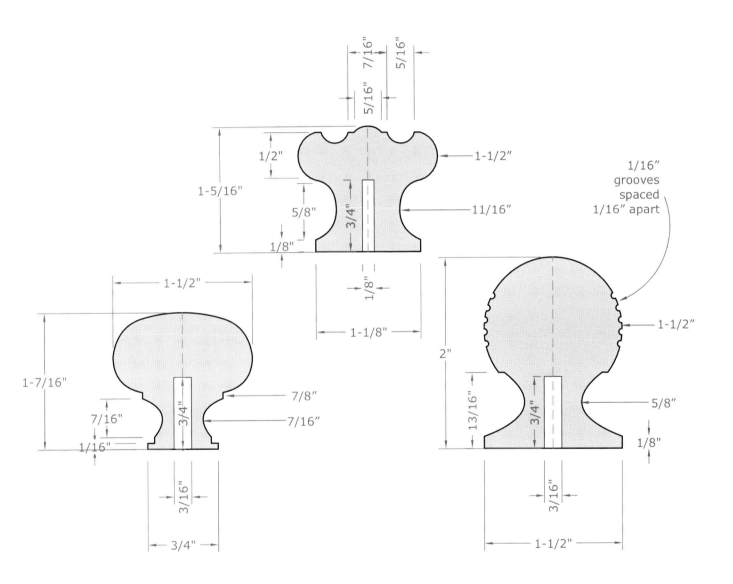

Knobs
& Finials

BOX FINIAL I

This easily turned finial makes a big impact on the look of a small turned box. The best way to turn it is to choose a blank that's 1-1/2 in. square and 3 in. long. Grip one end in a scroll chuck and bring up the tailstock to support the work. The tailstock end will be the tip of the finial. Work from the tailstock toward the headstock to shape the piece, then carefully part it off.

BOX FINIAL I

Photocopy pattern at 33.33% for actual size.

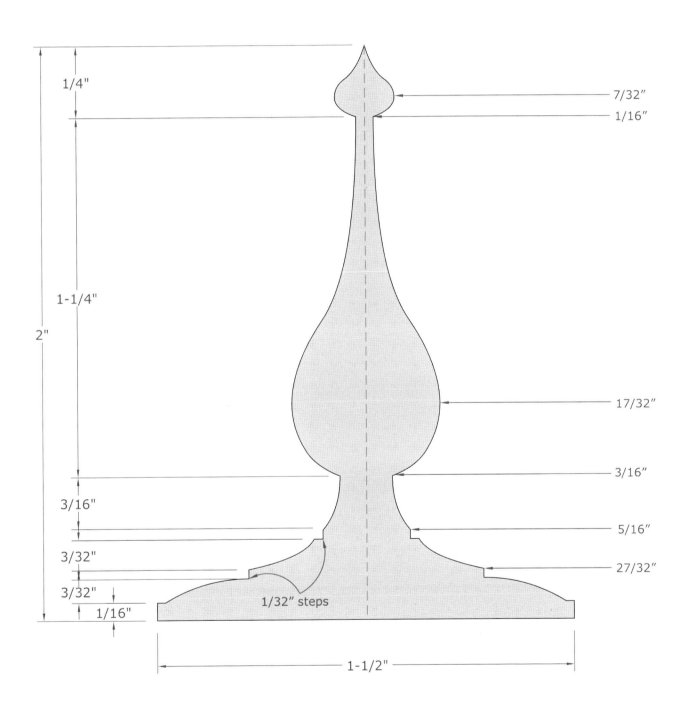

1/4"

1-1/4"

2"

3/16"

3/32"

3/32"

1/16"

1/32" steps

1-1/2"

7/32"

1/16"

17/32"

3/16"

5/16"

27/32"

BOX FINIAL II

The length of this finial and its thinness combine to make it a challenging piece of spindle turning.

Use a close-grained wood like hard maple or blackwood. Make the blank about an inch longer than the finial. Hold it in a scroll chuck and advance the tailstock to support the blank. The tailstock end will be the tip of the finial. Shape the piece by working from the tailstock toward the headstock, supporting the work with your free hand.

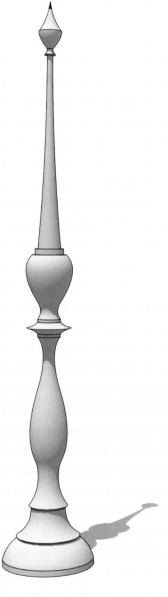

BOX FINIAL II

Photocopy pattern at 100% for actual size.

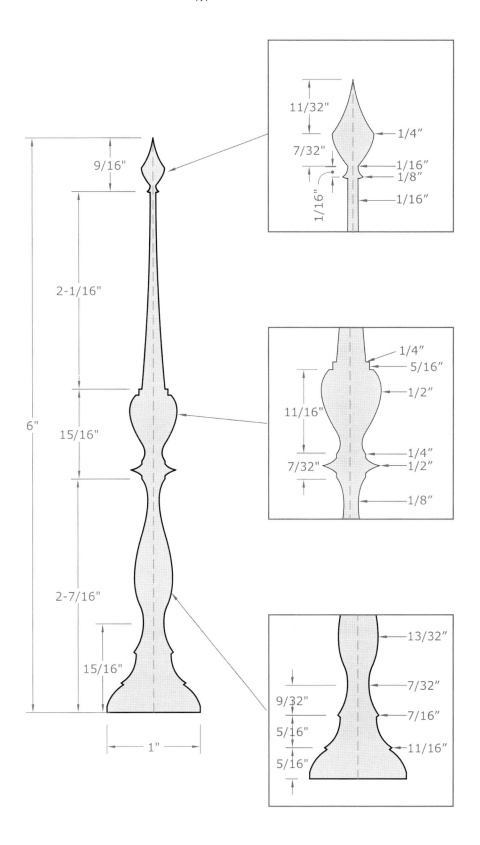

A PAIR OF FURNITURE FINIALS

The dimensions for these finials were culled from *Heirloom Furniture,* a classic book of plans by Franklin H. Gottschall, published in 1957.

The finial on the left was intended for the posts on a four-poster bed. The one one the right comes from the pediment on a Governor Winthrop secretary. Both finials have a tenon that fits into a hole in a rectangular base. The top of the Governor Winthrop finial is shown as a plain teardrop shape, but you could carve it with spiral flutes to make it a flame finial.

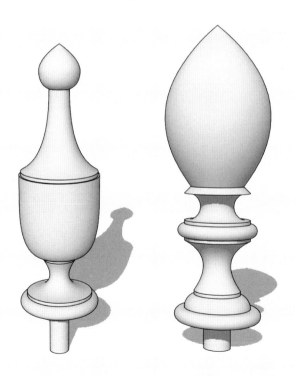

A PAIR OF
FURNITURE FINIALS

Photocopy pattern at 100% for actual size.

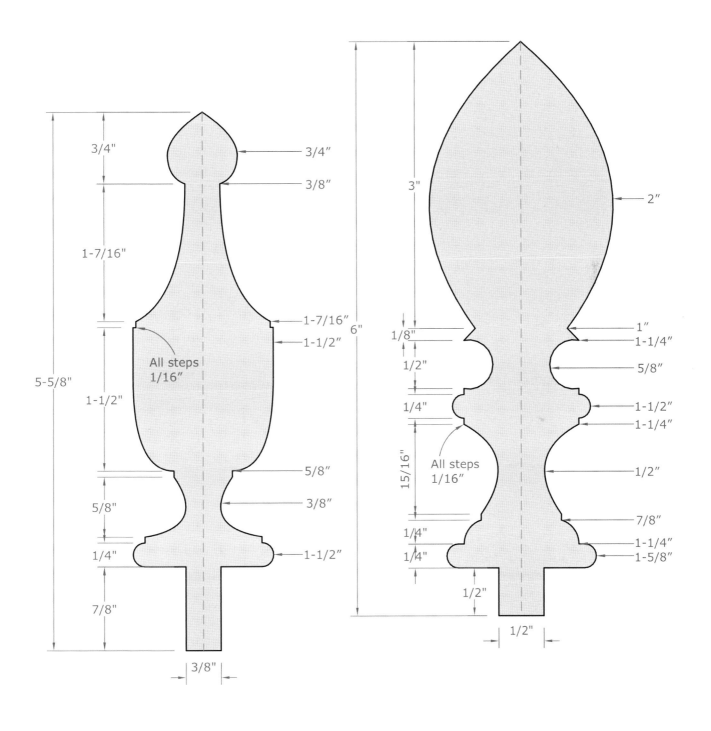

PATTERNS

CHAPTER

4

Shop & Garden

If you have tools, you need handles. Turning tools, for example, are often sold without a handle, leaving you free to make your own. It's easy to shape a round handle, but you may want to try a more challenging three-sided handle.

You can buy kits for making the handle on a multi-tip screwdriver, scratch awl, or various other tools. And there are useful tools you can make from scratch, such as a hefty hardwood mallet or a bulb-planting tool known as a garden dibble.

THREE-SIDED TOOL HANDLE

This handle was designed for lathe tools, but it would work just as well on any number of shop tools. Turning this one is an exercise in multi-axis turning. That is, you mount the blank on four different sets of centers to shape the sides.

Mill a blank exactly 1-1/2 in. square and an inch longer than you want the handle to be. Make two copies of the pattern for locating centers, on the facing page, and paste one on each end of the blank. Mount the blank on the true center and turn it round. Then remount it on the numbered centers in turn and cut down to the line on the pattern at the tailstock end. Leave an inch at the headstock end for remounting the blank. You will be turning mostly air. With the lathe off, sand the faces smooth.

Grab the blank in a scroll chuck and shape the end as needed for a ferrule, a hole for the tool, or both. Round over the ends and part off the handle.

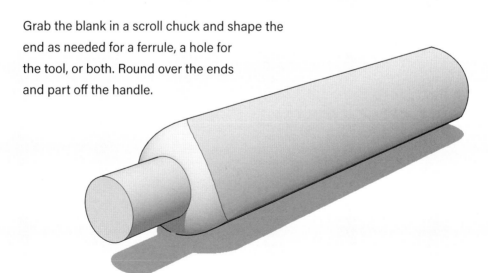

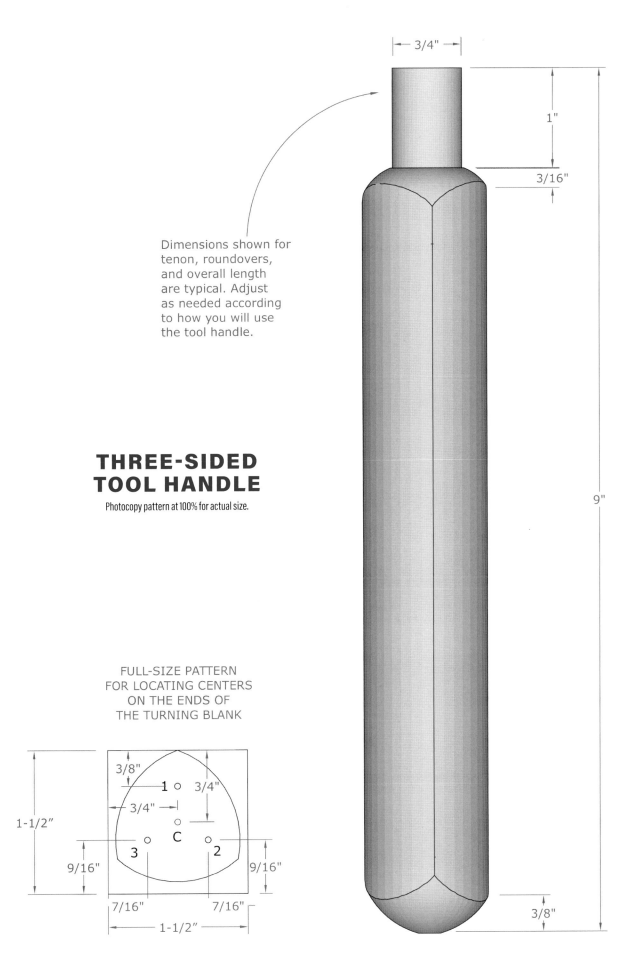

3/4"

1"

3/16"

Dimensions shown for tenon, roundovers, and overall length are typical. Adjust as needed according to how you will use the tool handle.

9"

THREE-SIDED TOOL HANDLE

Photocopy pattern at 100% for actual size.

FULL-SIZE PATTERN
FOR LOCATING CENTERS
ON THE ENDS OF
THE TURNING BLANK

3/8"

3/8"

1 ○   3/4"

3/4"

1-1/2"

C

3   2

9/16"

9/16"

7/16"   7/16"

1-1/2"

SCREWDRIVER HANDLE

Several woodworking retailers offer kits for a 4-in-1 or 6-in-1 screwdriver. The kits are generally the same: An insert, or bolster, is epoxied into the turned handle and holds a reversible shaft with straight and Phillips bits on each end. But each kit is slightly different. Bolsters aren't all the same size; some kits come with a ferrule, but others don't.

The handle shown here actually requires very little turning. When you cut the turning blank, use the tablesaw to make it six-sided. Cut it about an inch longer than the finished handle and grip one end in a scroll chuck. Drill the stepped hole, following the instructions that come with your screwdriver kit. Round the ends and lightly sand the rest of the handle to ease the edges. Part it off and glue the bolster in place.

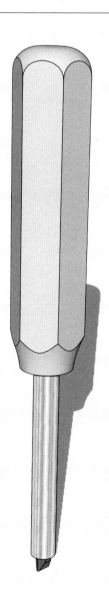

SCREWDRIVER HANDLE

Photocopy pattern at 100% for actual size.

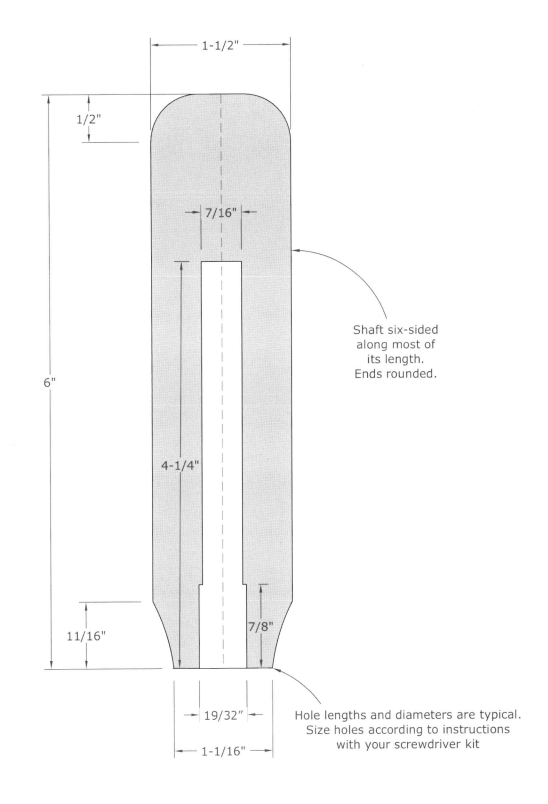

1-1/2"

1/2"

7/16"

6"

4-1/4"

Shaft six-sided
along most of
its length.
Ends rounded.

11/16"

7/8"

19/32"

1-1/16"

Hole lengths and diameters are typical.
Size holes according to instructions
with your screwdriver kit

ONE-PIECE MALLET

To make a long-lasting mallet, look for a good, dry, straight-grained billet of a durable hardwood like hard maple or lignum vitae. This piece will get a lot of use and abuse, so you'll want a wood that's up to the job.

Feel free to adjust the shape of the handle as you turn the mallet to be sure it fits your hand comfortably. Turning a good chamfer on the top of the mallet helps prevent the wood from splitting after an errant blow.

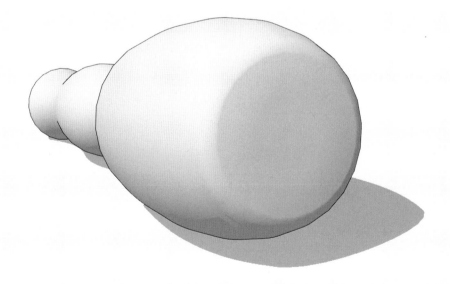

ONE-PIECE
MALLET

Photocopy pattern at 133% for actual size.

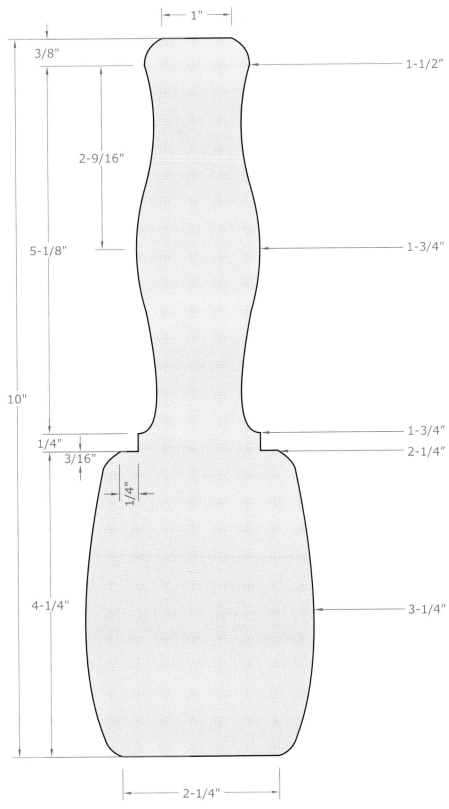

1"

3/8"

1-1/2"

2-9/16"

1-3/4"

5-1/8"

10"

1-3/4"

2-1/4"

1/4"

3/16"

1/4"

4-1/4"

3-1/4"

2-1/4"

CHISEL HANDLE, TWO STYLES

Chisels that have a socket on the end of the blade for the handle are generally known as firmer chisels. Mortising chisels often have a metal hoop at the end of the handle, to prevent the wood from mushrooming under repeated blows from a mallet.

The pattern on the left is for a basic firmer chisel handle. The pattern on the right modifies the end of the handle to accommodate a metal hoop.

Use the dimensions on the patterns as guidelines. Adjust them as needed so the handle fits snugly in the socket, and so the shape fits your hand comfortably.

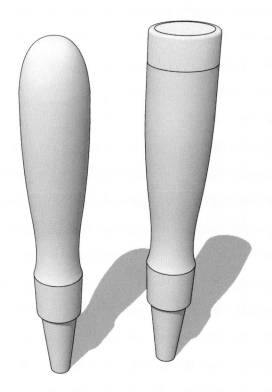

CHISEL HANDLE, TWO STYLES

Photocopy pattern at 100% for actual size.

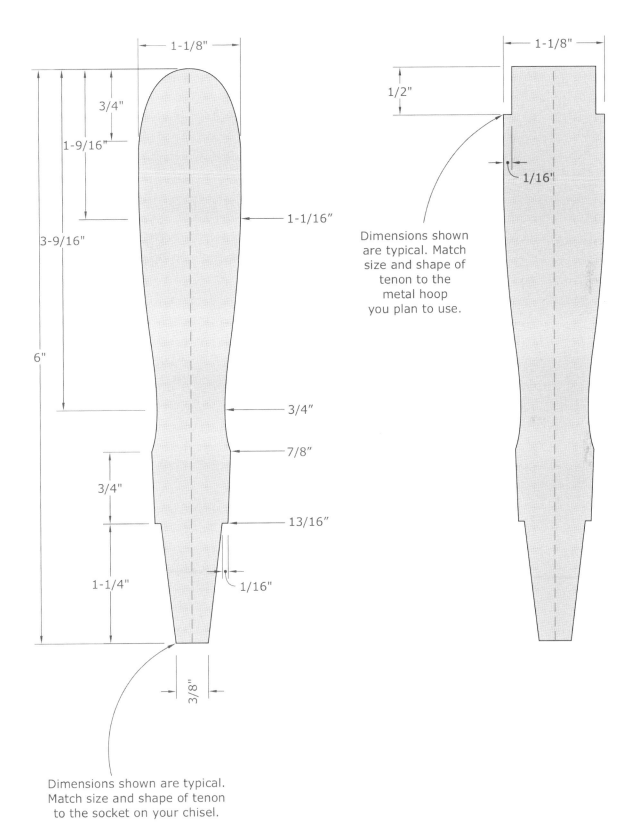

1-1/8"

3/4"

1-9/16"

3-9/16"

1-1/16"

6"

3/4"

7/8"

3/4"

13/16"

1-1/4"

1/16"

3/8"

Dimensions shown are typical. Match size and shape of tenon to the socket on your chisel.

1-1/8"

1/2"

1/16"

Dimensions shown are typical. Match size and shape of tenon to the metal hoop you plan to use.

SCRATCH AWL HANDLE

A good awl will be a prized workshop go-to for years to come. The classic turning shown here is comfortable in your hand and could be easily adapted to fit any kit.

Some high-end toolmakers make absolutely gorgeous awls using highly figured tropical hardwoods. You can do the same with the awl handle you turn.

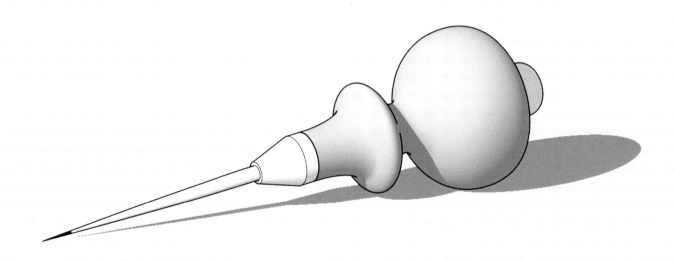

SCRATCH AWL
HANDLE

Photocopy pattern at 50% for actual size.

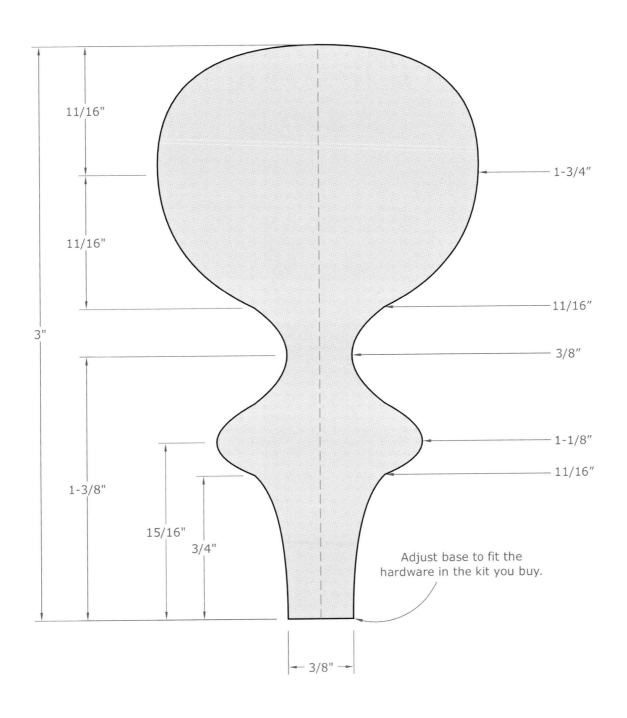

11/16"

11/16"

3"

1-3/8"

15/16"

3/4"

3/8"

1-3/4"

11/16"

3/8"

1-1/8"

11/16"

Adjust base to fit the
hardware in the kit you buy.

GARDEN DIBBLE

Gardeners have long used dibbles (also known as dibbers) to punch uniform holes in the soil for planting bulbs and seedlings. Many dibbles, including the one shown here, have grooves every inch along the shaft. They help you gauge how deep to drive the dibble.

You can use just about any hardwood for this tool. Maple, cherry, mahogany, and teak would would all be good choices.

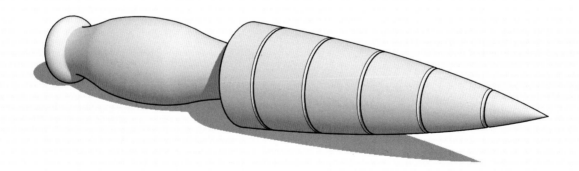

GARDEN
DIBBLE

Photocopy pattern at 133% for actual size.

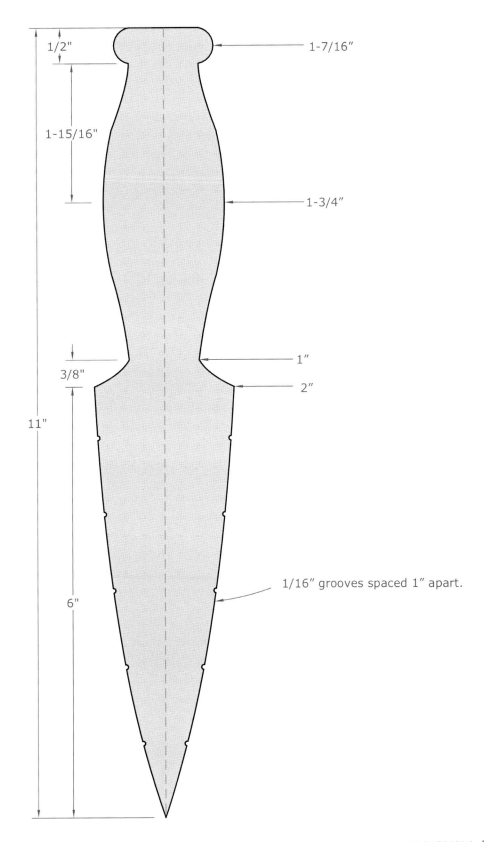

1/2"

1-7/16"

1-15/16"

1-3/4"

1"

2"

3/8"

11"

6"

1/16" grooves spaced 1" apart.

PATTERNS

Lamps & Candlesticks

Candlesticks and lamp bases don't have to be made from glass, ceramic, silver, brass, or pewter. And a turned one can be given a natural finish or made to resemble those other materials by finishing it with gold or silver leaf or with a high-gloss paint.

For the most part, the candlesticks are straightforward spindle turnings. The lamp bases are probably best turned from a blank assembled from several smaller pieces. The Art Deco lamp base (see page 106) is designed as a segmented turning.

The patterns show holes in the center of the lamp bases for the cord, a threaded rod, or both. Give the lamp even more of a personal touch by choosing your own lamp hardware and shade.

OSOLNIK-STYLE CANDLESTICK

Rude Osolnik (1915–2001) was one of the giants of woodturning in the mid-20th century. Along with Bob Stocksdale (see page 136) and Ed Moulthrop, Osolnik helped elevate turning from utilitarian handiwork to fine art. He taught at Berea College, in Kentucky, for 40 years, and gave lessons and demonstrations across the U.S.

Many of Osolnik's pieces are in the permanent collections of leading galleries and museums. The candlestick shown here is based on one of his signature pieces. He made the candlestick in several sizes. The 9-1/2 in. version is one of the tallest.

When you turn this piece, choose a wood like mahogany or teak, with a blank about an inch longer than the finished candlestick. Turn the blank round and shape a tenon on one end so you can grip the blank in a scroll chuck. Drill the hole for the candle and shape the top of the piece. Use the tailstock and your free hand to support the work as you complete the profile.

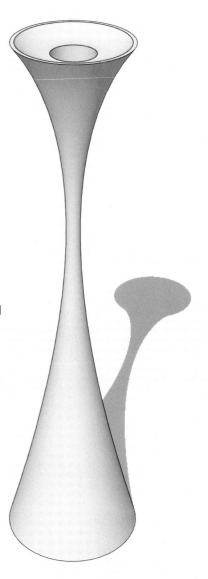

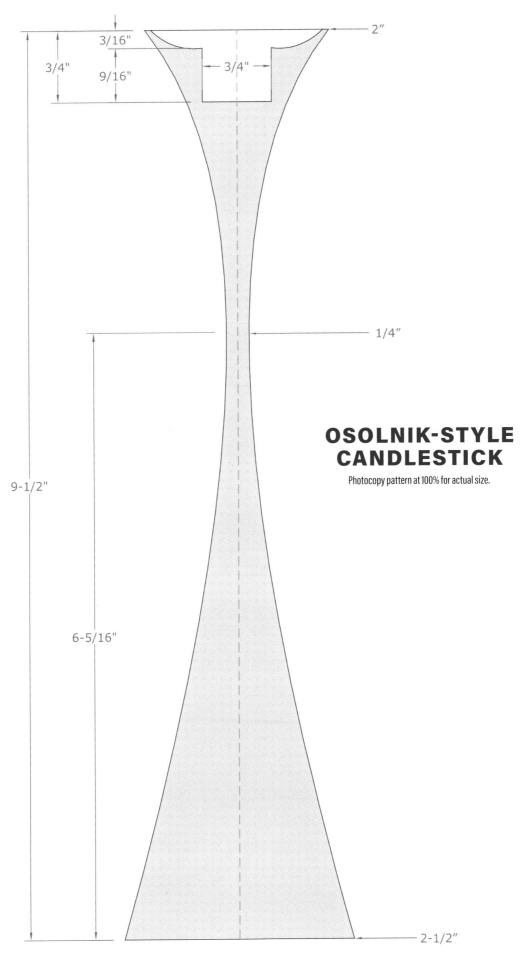

2″

3/16″

3/4″

9/16″

3/4″

1/4″

**OSOLNIK-STYLE
CANDLESTICK**

Photocopy pattern at 100% for actual size.

9-1/2″

6-5/16″

2-1/2″

TRADITIONAL CANDLESTICK

With curves, beads, and coves that aren't especially intricate, this modest-sized piece is fairly easy to turn. Feel free to modify the design by turning a single bead under the candle cup, say, or modifying the curve on the base.

The bowl requires a blank measuring at least 9 in. long and 4-1/2 in. square. You can use just about any wood for this project.

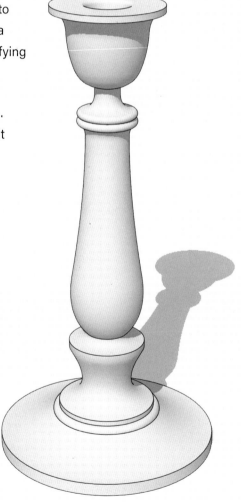

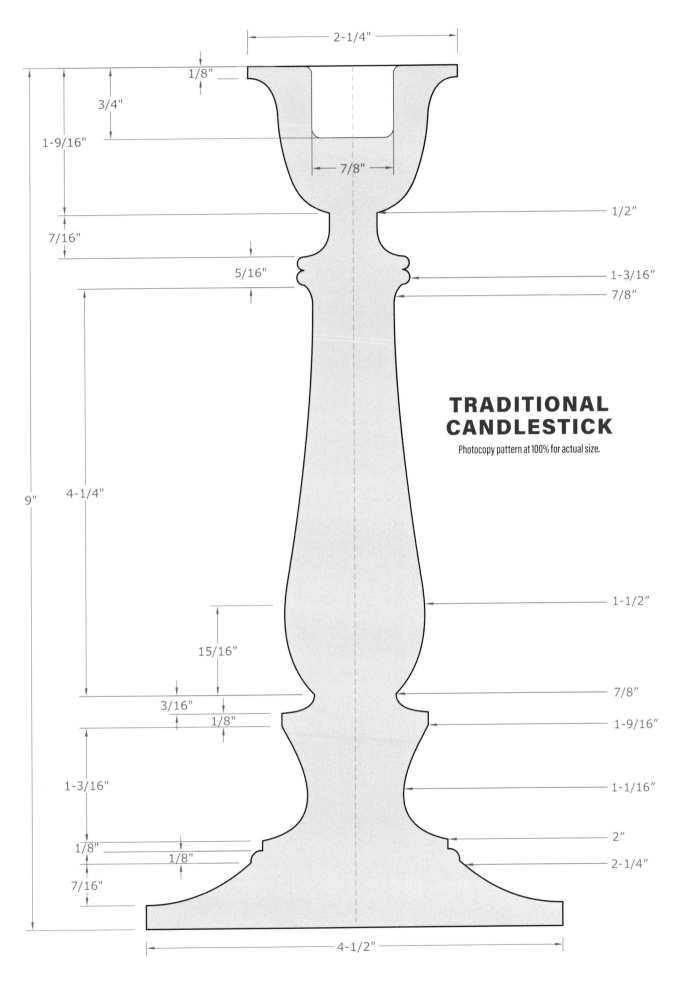

2-1/4"

1/8"

3/4"

1-9/16"

7/8"

1/2"

7/16"

5/16"

1-3/16"

7/8"

TRADITIONAL
CANDLESTICK

Photocopy pattern at 100% for actual size.

9"

4-1/4"

1-1/2"

15/16"

3/16"

1/8"

7/8"

1-9/16"

1-3/16"

1-1/16"

1/8"

1/8"

2"

2-1/4"

7/16"

4-1/2"

NEOCLASSICAL CANDLESTICK

This tall candlestick would look at home solo atop a dining table or displayed as part of a small collection. When turning this elegant design, do your best to keep beads and details crisp.

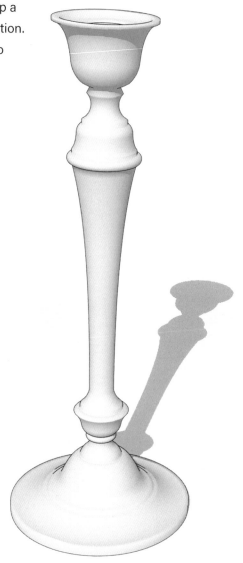

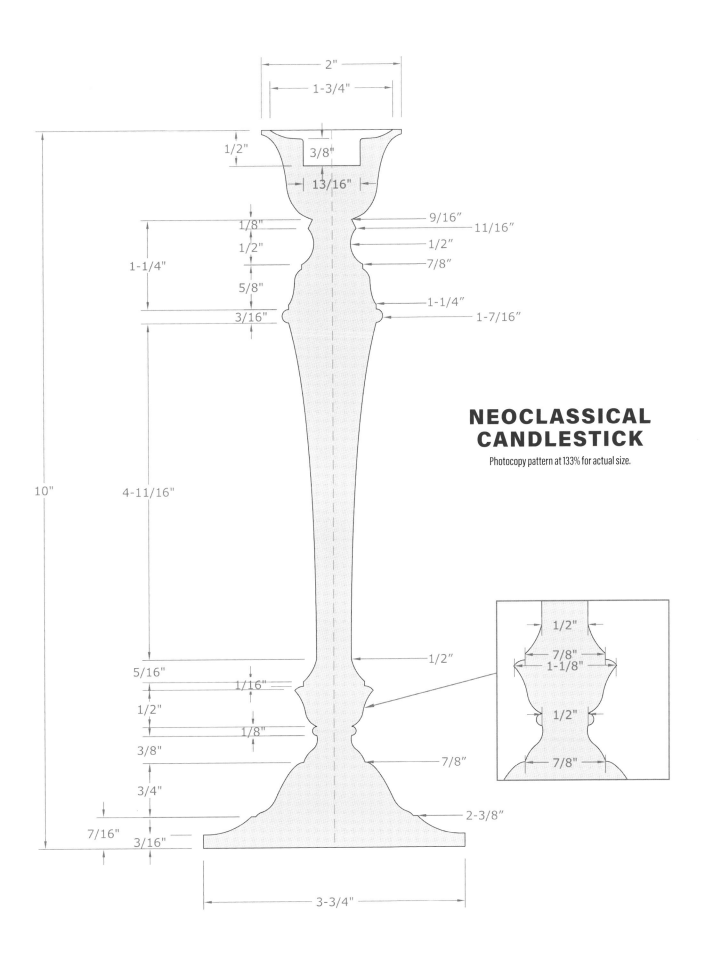

NEOCLASSICAL CANDLESTICK

Photocopy pattern at 133% for actual size.

Lamps & Candlesticks

ROBERT JARVIE DELTA CANDLESTICK

Robert Jarvie was a jeweler and metalsmith who worked in Chicago in the early 20th century. In his relatively brief career, he produced some extraordinary Arts & Crafts candlestick designs. He used the Greek alphabet to identify his pieces; this is the Delta design.

The long, thin shaft makes this a challenging piece to turn. Orient the workpiece so the candle cup is at the tailstock end of the lathe. Keep the work supported at the tailstock end and along the shaft. To conserve wood, you may want to turn the base separately, with a hole in the center to accept a tenon on the end of the shaft.

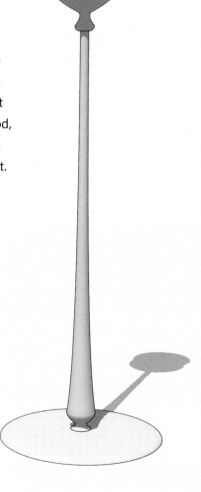

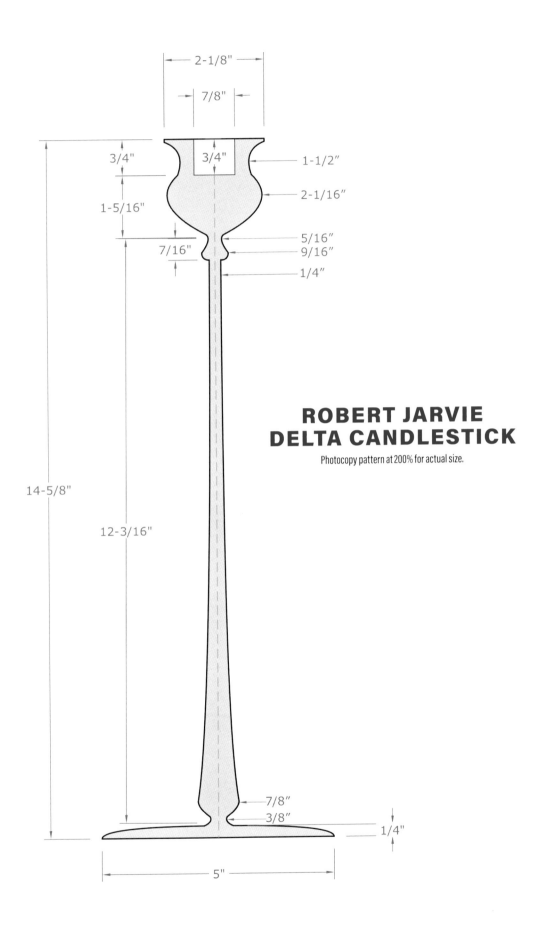

2-1/8"

7/8"

3/4"   3/4"   1-1/2"

2-1/16"

1-5/16"

7/16"   5/16"
9/16"

1/4"

ROBERT JARVIE
DELTA CANDLESTICK
Photocopy pattern at 200% for actual size.

14-5/8"

12-3/16"

7/8"
3/8"

1/4"

5"

ROBERT JARVIE LAMBDA CANDLESTICK

Here's another of Jarvie's designs. This one should be much easier to turn than the one shown on the previous page.

You may want to make the wide base separately from the rest of the candlestick, then glue the parts together. Shape the curve at the base after the two pieces have been joined.

Either Jarvie candlestick would look great finished with a high-gloss black lacquer. Or, consider gilding them with a copper leaf or mica powder. A quick Internet search will steer you to good sources of gilding supplies and instruction.

ROBERT JARVIE
LAMBDA CANDLESTICK

Photocopy pattern at 100% for actual size.

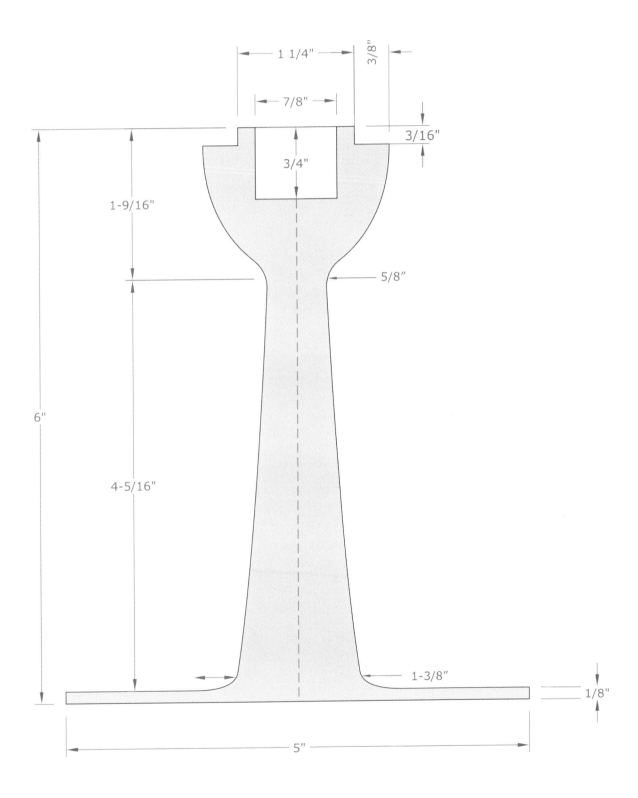

TABLE LAMP BASE IN THE ART DECO STYLE

The center portion of this design is a segmented turning. Build up the turning blank by gluing together 12 wedge-shaped staves, with a thin strip of contrasting wood between each stave. The combinations are endless: Rosewood staves separated by holly strips, or zebrawood separated by blackwood are just two possibilities. You could even use aluminum or brass for the accent strips. Make the cap and the base from a third wood that complements the others.

Making the center of the base as a segmented turning leaves the middle open, so you can add a threaded rod for the lamp cord without having to drill a foot-long hole in the piece.

Turn the center, base, and cap separately. Glue the pieces together, remount the assembly between centers, and true it up.

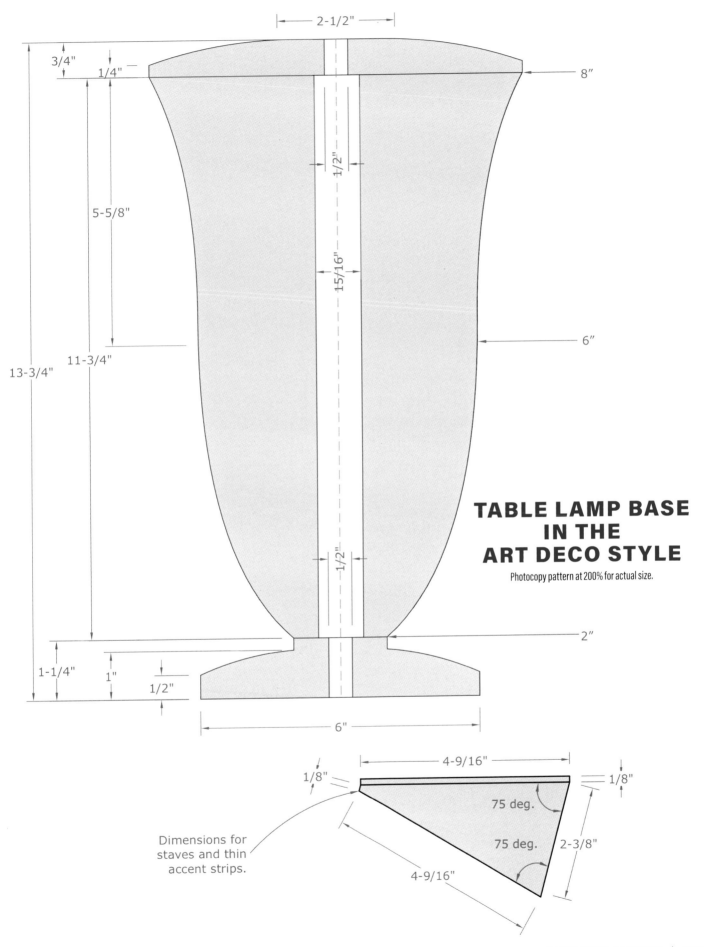

2-1/2"

3/4"
1/4"
8"

1/2"

5-5/8"

15/16"

6"

13-3/4"

11-3/4"

TABLE LAMP BASE
IN THE
ART DECO STYLE

Photocopy pattern at 200% for actual size.

1/2"

2"

1-1/4"

1"

1/2"

6"

4-9/16"

1/8"

1/8"

75 deg.

75 deg.

2-3/8"

Dimensions for
staves and thin
accent strips.

4-9/16"

MIDCENTURY MODERN TABLE LAMP BASE

You may find it easier to turn this bulbous shape in two parts. Make the 9-in.-diameter bottom part first; drill the center as shown to leave room for a threaded rod and the lamp cord. Turn the narrow neck next. Glue the halves together, then remount the piece between centers and refine the shape to obscure the seam.

You can turn this lamp base from a wood like mahogany or bubinga. You could use white oak, finished by scorching the wood with a propane torch and burnishing it with a wire brush. Or, you could use a plain wood such as poplar and finish it with milk paint.

MIDCENTURY MODERN
TABLE LAMP BASE

Photocopy pattern at 200% for actual size.

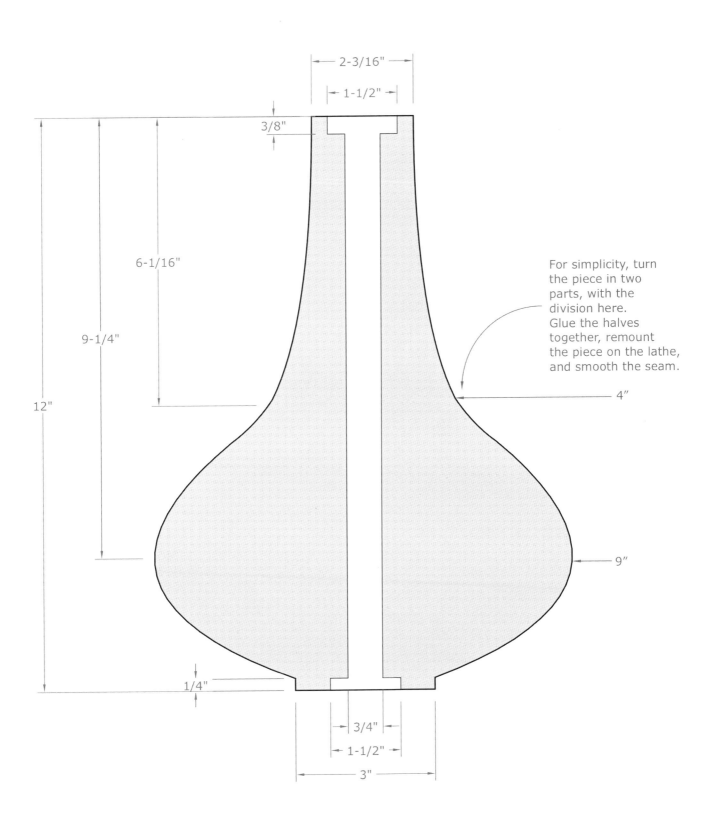

2-3/16"

1-1/2"

3/8"

6-1/16"

9-1/4"

12"

For simplicity, turn
the piece in two
parts, with the
division here.
Glue the halves
together, remount
the piece on the lathe,
and smooth the seam.

4"

9"

1/4"

3/4"

1-1/2"

3"

GINGER JAR
TABLE LAMP BASE

This design can be turned from a single piece of wood or a from a blank glued up from layers of flat stock to create a workpiece that measures 10-1/2 x 10-1/2 in. Drill the center hole as you go, keeping the blanks aligned with a dowel.

GINGER JAR
TABLE LAMP BASE

Photocopy pattern at 200% for actual size.

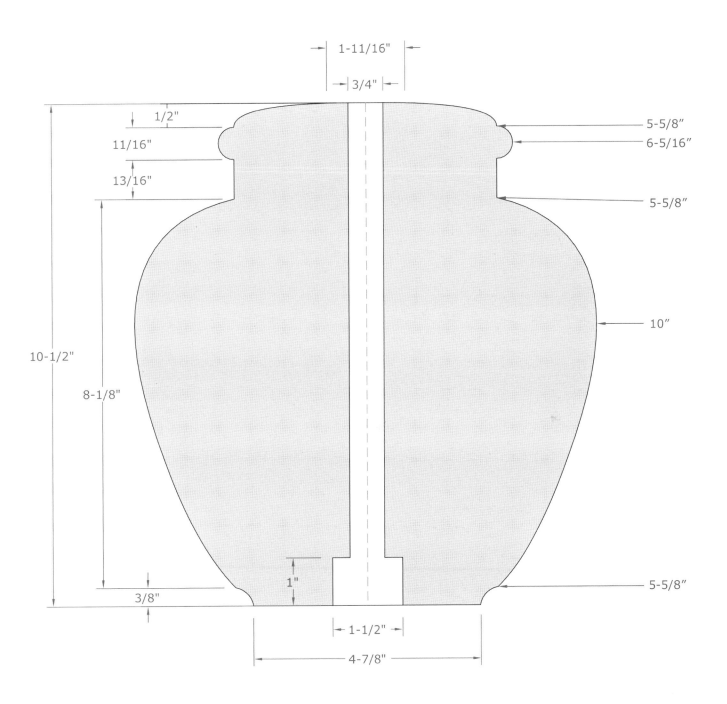

PATTERNS

Bowls, Vases & Platters

The homes of many turners are filled with empty bowls. For them, making a bowl is an end in itself; you don't have to fill the bowl to enjoy it. Not everyone feels that way, though. Mike Mahoney, one of the best woodturners working today, eats off plates, platters, and bowls that he has made. For him and many others, a bowl exists to be used.

Whether you want a utilitarian piece or one just for its looks, you'll find a variety of shapes, sizes, and styles to suit your tastes.

A BASIC
BOWL

This no-nonsense design makes a perfect bowl for your morning breakfast cereal—it fits nicely in the hand (and holds a lot of Cheerios) and could be proudly displayed when not in use. The classic bowl shape makes it an attractive, useful piece that's also pretty easy to turn.

The bowl requires a blank measuring 6 in. in diameter and 3-1/2 in. thick, and just about any wood will work.

A BASIC BOWL

Photocopy pattern at 100% for actual size.

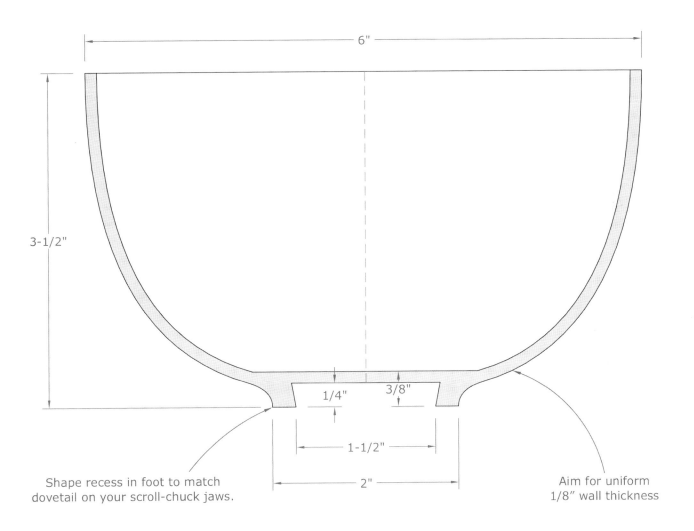

6"

3-1/2"

1/4"

3/8"

1-1/2"

2"

Shape recess in foot to match dovetail on your scroll-chuck jaws.

Aim for uniform 1/8" wall thickness

BOWL WITH ROLLED RIM

This straightforward bowl design is a favorite shape of the renowned actor and hobbyist woodturner William H. Macy.

Macy, best known for his portrayal of Frank Gallagher on the Showtime series "Shameless," began woodturning when he was shooting the film "Fargo." Now, when he has enough spare time, he retreats to his shop to do some cabinetmaking or woodturning.

The bowl's rim consists of a large bead that blends seamlessly into the interior. The wall curves from the rim to a plain, straight foot. At 9 in. in diameter and 3 in. tall, the piece is relatively small. You can easily translate the shape to a larger or smaller blank.

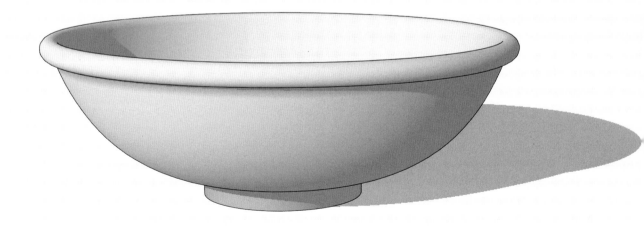

BOWL WITH ROLLED RIM

Photocopy pattern at 133% for actual size.

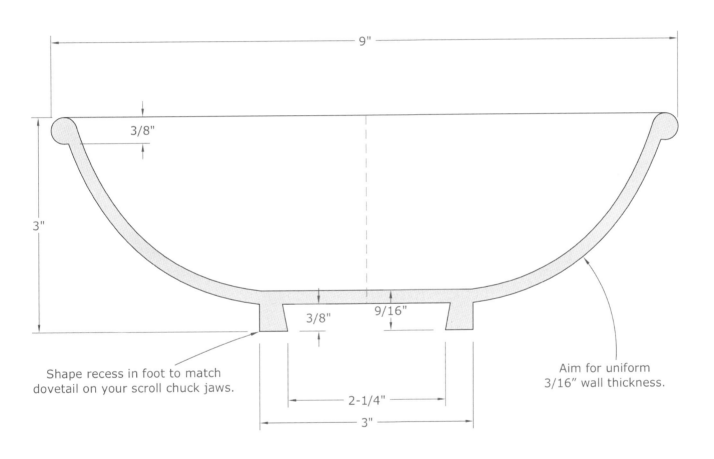

9"

3/8"

3"

9/16"

3/8"

Shape recess in foot to match
dovetail on your scroll chuck jaws.

Aim for uniform
3/16" wall thickness.

2-1/4"

3"

REVERE-STYLE BOWL

First created in silver by Revolutionary icon Paul Revere, the timeless lines of this bowl translate well into wood.

You will need a blank measuring 5-3/4 in. high and 10 in. in diameter. If you can't find a piece of wood that size, turn the base separately from the rest of the piece. Glue the turned parts together once they are sanded but before they are finished.

REVERE-STYLE
BOWL

Photocopy pattern at 200% for actual size.

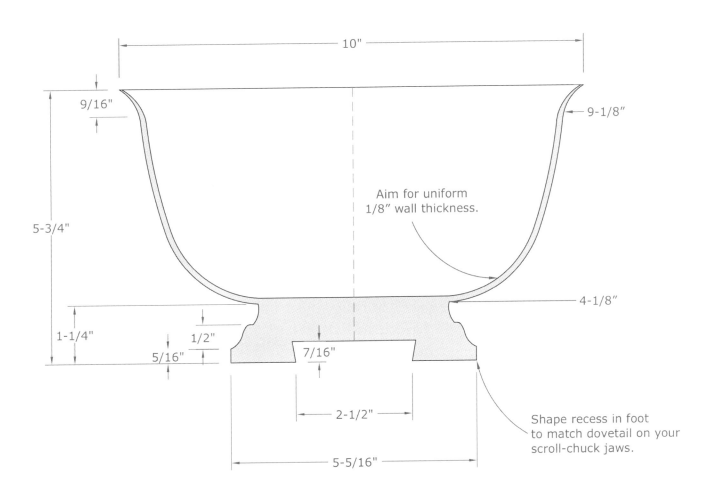

10"

9/16"

9-1/8"

Aim for uniform
1/8" wall thickness.

5-3/4"

4-1/8"

1-1/4"

1/2"

5/16"

7/16"

2-1/2"

5-5/16"

Shape recess in foot
to match dovetail on your
scroll-chuck jaws.

CALABASH-STYLE BOWL

Turning this shape presents a bit of a challenge because of the way the side curves inward toward the rim. Shaping the inside of the bowl requires some careful work with a scraper or a hollowing tool.

Begin with a blank measuring 3 in. high and 6 in. in diameter. Consider using a strikingly figured wood like spalted ambrosia maple, maple or cherry burl, red gum, or flame box elder.

If you use the base of the bowl as a tenon for a scroll chuck, you will have to do some clean-up at the end to turn or sand away marks left by the chuck jaws. To avoid that, turn a dovetail recess in the base for the chuck.

CALABASH-STYLE BOWL

Photocopy pattern at 100% for actual size.

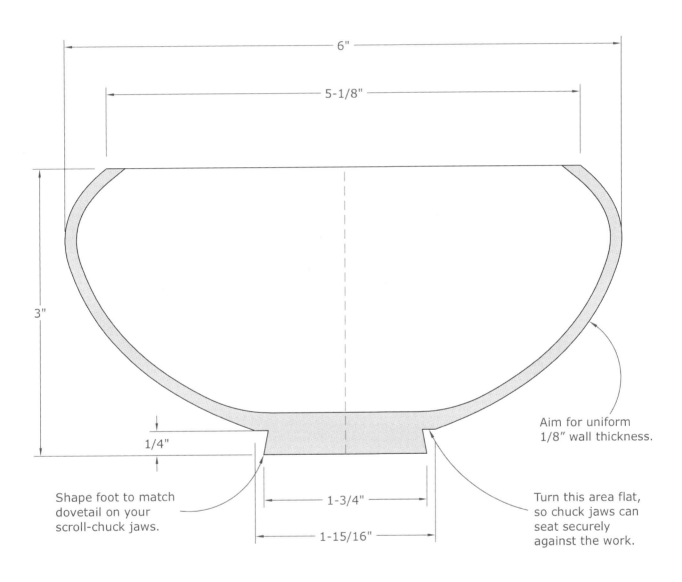

6"

5-1/8"

3"

1/4"

Aim for uniform 1/8" wall thickness.

1-3/4"

1-15/16"

Shape foot to match dovetail on your scroll-chuck jaws.

Turn this area flat, so chuck jaws can seat securely against the work.

URUSHI-STYLE BOWL

Urushi is a distinctive lacquer used in traditional Japanese crafts. A bowl like the one shown here would be finished with multiple coats of urushi.

If you want to turn this bowl and use it at mealtime, avoid lacquer and give it a food-safe finish, such as walnut oil or mineral oil. After use, wipe it clean with a damp cloth, but keep it out of the dishpan and dishwasher.

When turned in cherry, this design ages beautifully over the years, turning a deep pecan brown. That said, most any hardwood would be an appropriate choice for this one.

URUSHI-STYLE
BOWL

Photocopy pattern at 100% for actual size.

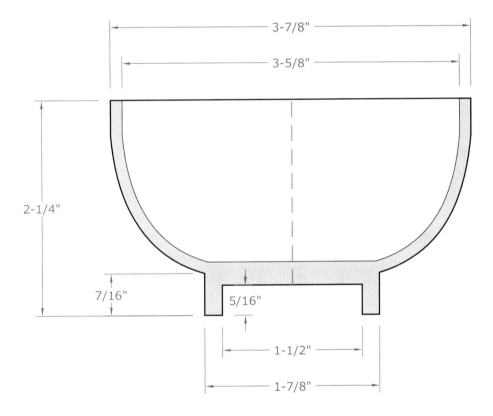

3-7/8"

3-5/8"

2-1/4"

7/16"

5/16"

1-1/2"

1-7/8"

A BASIC BOX WITH LID

Typically, a turned box and lid are made from the same piece of wood, so that the grain pattern appears to flow seamlessly from top to base.

Making a lidded box involves rechucking the work several times. Here's one way to do that: Mount the blank between centers and turn a tenon for a scroll chuck. Remount the piece, holding it by that tenon. Shape the outside of the base and the recess at the foot. Part off the base. Remount the base, holding it in a scroll chuck, to finish the inside and the lip at the rim. Remove the base and mount the lid, holding it by the tenon. Shape the inside, checking the work carefully to be sure the lid fits tightly on the base. Reverse the lid, gripping it in the scroll chuck, to finish the outside.

A BASIC
BOX WITH LID

Photocopy pattern at 100% for actual size.

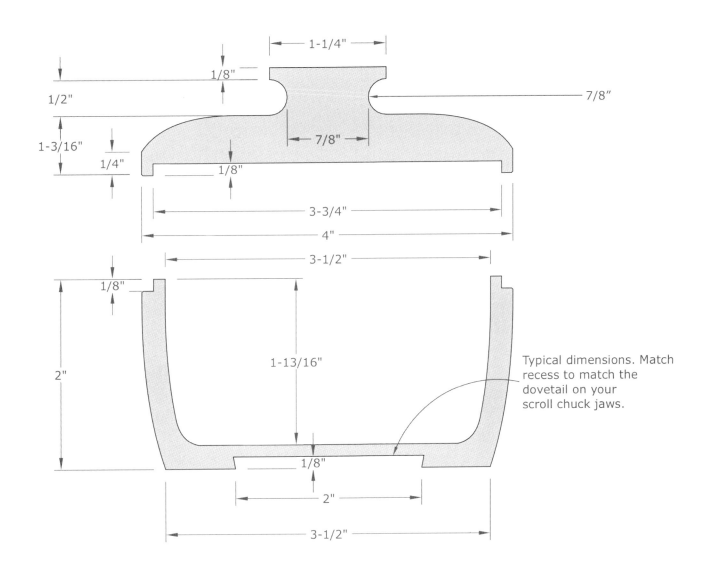

1-1/4"

1/8"

1/2"

7/8"

1-3/16"

1/4"

7/8"

1/8"

1/8"

3-3/4"

4"

3-1/2"

1/8"

1-13/16"

2"

Typical dimensions. Match recess to match the dovetail on your scroll chuck jaws.

1/8"

2"

3-1/2"

WEED POT

A weed pot makes a good project for beginners, mainly because most of the work goes to shaping the outside. You don't have to hollow the inside completely—just drill the opening and shape the flare at the top.

You will need a blank measuring a little more than 6 in. long and 3 in. square. Mount it between centers, turn it round, and shape a tenon at one end. Remount the blank, this time holding the tenon in a scroll chuck. Drill out the center, as shown in the pattern, with a Jacobs chuck in the tailstock. Replace the Jacobs chuck with a cone center and bring the tailstock up so the center presses into the center hole. Shape the outside of the weed pot to your liking. Retract the cone center so you can shape the top of the piece. When you've finished, part off the weed pot.

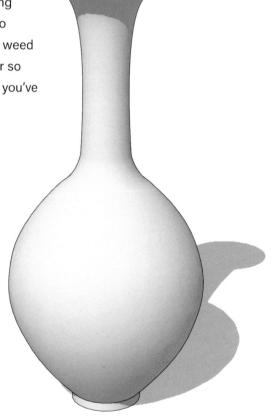

WEED POT

Photocopy pattern at 100% for actual size.

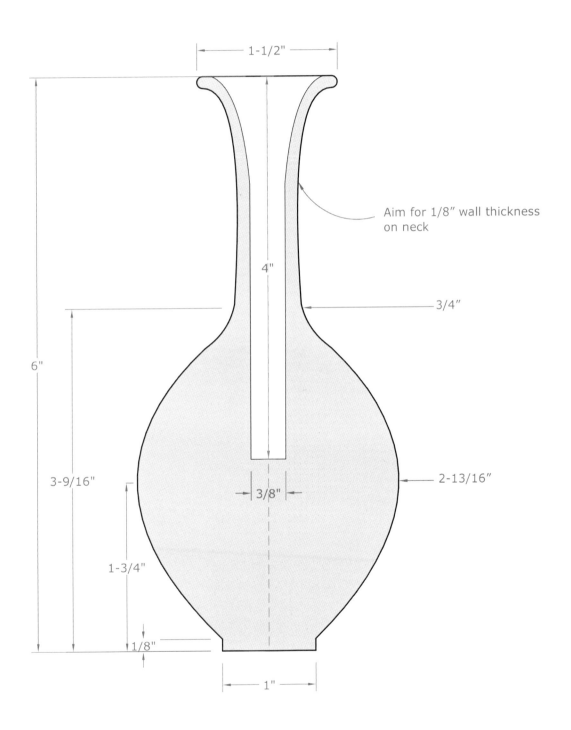

1-1/2"

Aim for 1/8" wall thickness on neck

4"

3/4"

6"

3-9/16"

3/8"

2-13/16"

1-3/4"

1/8"

1"

SMALL VASE

This small vase is sometimes referred to as a dahlia vase, but it's not just for those blooms—you can use it for any kind of fresh or dried flower.

This piece is best turned by shaping a tenon on one end of the blank, then gripping the piece by that tenon in a scroll chuck. Once you have shaped and hollowed the vase, part off the tenon.

SMALL VASE

Photocopy pattern at 100% for actual size.

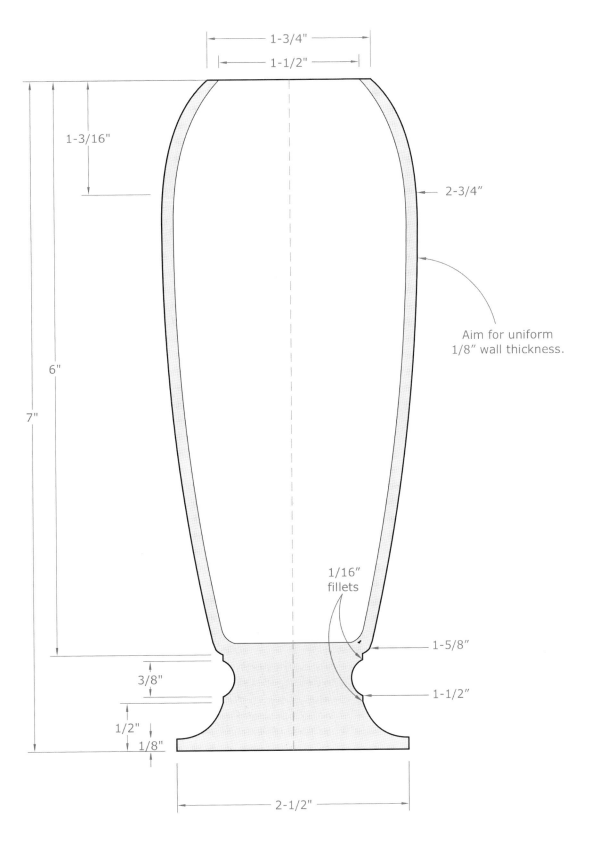

1-3/4"

1-1/2"

1-3/16"

2-3/4"

Aim for uniform
1/8" wall thickness.

6"

7"

1/16"
fillets

1-5/8"

3/8"

1-1/2"

1/2"

1/8"

2-1/2"

BASIC PLATTER

This design has all the necessary elements for a turned platter: A large, shallow recess in the center, a wide base for stability, and a generous rim to make the platter easy to hold.

Make this large piece from a wood with outstanding grain and figure, such as spalted ambrosia maple, birdseye maple, or a nice cherry or redwood burl. Finish it with lacquer or wipe-on polyurethane.

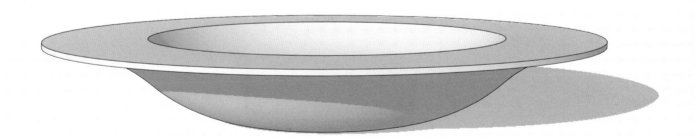

BASIC PLATTER

Photocopy pattern at 200% for actual size.

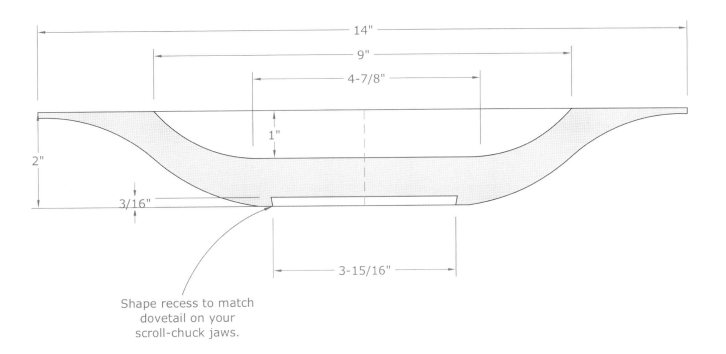

14"

9"

4-7/8"

1"

2"

3/16"

3-15/16"

Shape recess to match
dovetail on your
scroll-chuck jaws.

FLAT PLATTER

Slightly smaller than the platter on page 130, this piece has a rounded lip at the rim and a decorative profile on the base.

You could turn the platter from a plain wood like poplar, then finish it with several coats of high-gloss lacquer in fire-engine red, bright yellow, or black.

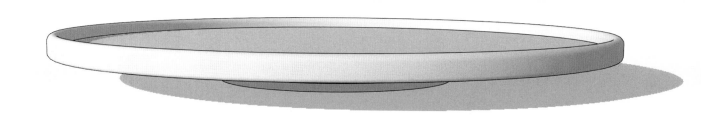

FLAT PLATTER

Photocopy pattern at 200% for actual size.

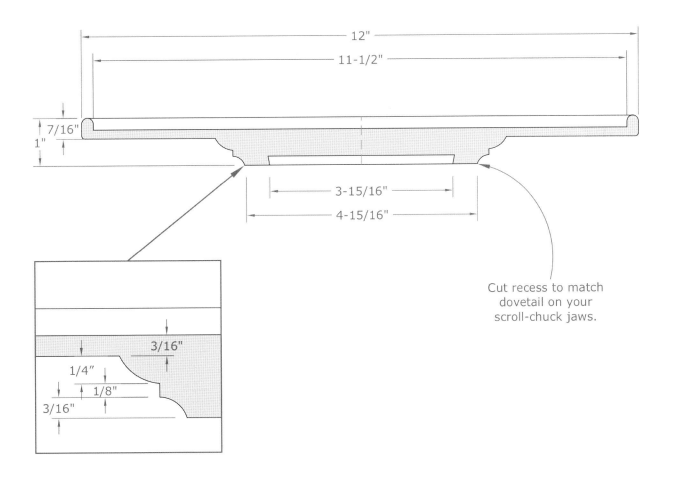

12"

11-1/2"

7/16"

1"

3-15/16"

4-15/16"

Cut recess to match
dovetail on your
scroll-chuck jaws.

3/16"

1/4"

1/8"

3/16"

Bowls, Vases & Platters

PLATTER INSPIRED BY RICHARD RAFFAN

Australian-based Richard Raffan is one of the world's best-known and most accomplished woodturners. This platter typifies his style. It is similar to the Basic Platter on page 130, but with subtle embellishments—the slightly undercut edge at the top, the generous curved rim, and the shallow beads in the recess at the foot.

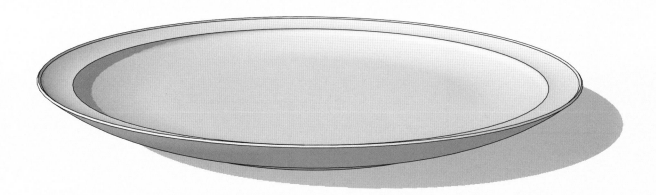

PLATTER INSPIRED
BY RICHARD RAFFAN

Photocopy pattern at 200% for actual size.

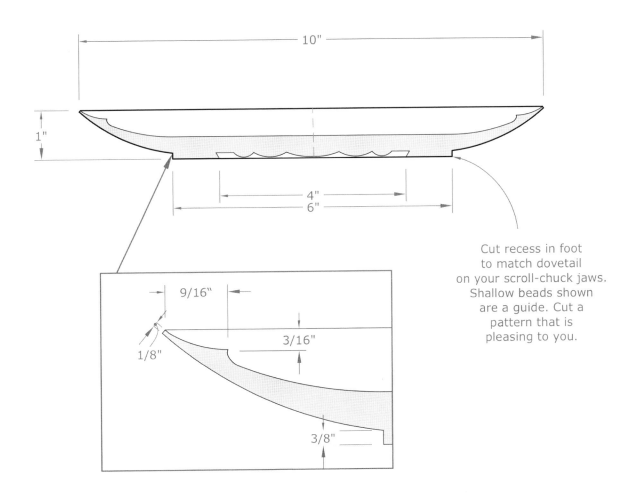

10"

1"

4"
6"

Cut recess in foot
to match dovetail
on your scroll-chuck jaws.
Shallow beads shown
are a guide. Cut a
pattern that is
pleasing to you.

9/16"

1/8"

3/16"

3/8"

SALAD SET INSPIRED BY BOB STOCKSDALE

Stocksdale (1913–2003) was one of the most influential woodturners of the mid-twentieth century. Like Rude Osolnik (see page 96), Stocksdale's work helped elevate turning from utilitarian craft to fine art. Ironically, though, he began his career by turning salad bowl sets, selling most of them through a San Francisco department store.

The inspiration for this set is a bowl that Stocksdale turned in 1982. The larger bowl requires a blank 15 in. in diameter and 6 in. thick. If you can't find a piece of wood that size, consider stacking two or three pieces of thinner stock and gluing them together. The smaller bowl requires a blank 7-1/2 in. in diameter and 4 in. thick.

SALAD SET INSPIRED BY
BOB STOCKSDALE

Photocopy Large Bowl pattern at 300% for actual size.
Photocopy Small Bowl pattern at 200% for actual size.

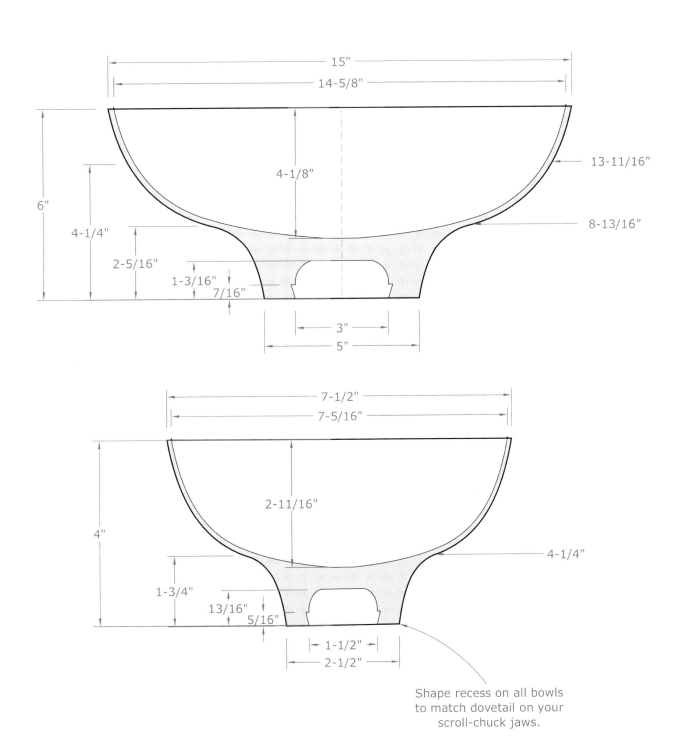

Shape recess on all bowls
to match dovetail on your
scroll-chuck jaws.

Resources

Lathes, tools, and accessories

Carter and Son Toolworks
carterandsontoolworks.com
206-878-7672

Carter Products
carterproducts.com
2871 Northridge Dr., NW
Grand Rapids, MI 49544
888-622-7837

Chucks Plus
chucksplus.com
15914 Mission Ridge
San Antonio, TX 78232
210-490-3754

John Jordan Woodturning
johnjordanwoodturning.com
6320 Burkitt Rd.
Cane Ridge, TN 37013
615-941-1247

Laguna Tools
lagunatools.com
2072 Alton Pkwy.
Irvine, CA 92606
Sales: 800-234-1976
Customer Service: 800-332-4094

Lyle Jamieson Woodturning LLC
lylejamieson.com
285 Lauri-Wil Ln.
Traverse City, MI 49696
231-947-2348

Oneway Manufacturing
oneway.ca
1-291 Griffith Rd.
Stratford, ON
N5A 6S4, Canada
800-565-7288

Robust Tools LLC
turnrobust.com
101 Business ID
Barneveld, WI 53507
866-630-1122

Thompson Lathe Tools
thompsonlathetools.com
5479 Columbia Rd.
N. Olmsted, OH 44070
440-241-6360

Trent Bosch Studios
trentbosch.com
10520 North County Rd. 17
Fort Collins, CO 80524
970-568-3299

Teknatool/Nova
novatoolsusa.com
4400 34th St. N., Unit M
St. Petersburg, FL 33714
866-748-3025

Vicmarc
vimarc.com
52 Grice St.,
Clontarf, Qld 4019 Australia
+61 7 3284 3103

Schools and classes

In addition to the schools and programs listed here, check the offerings at nearby community colleges, vocational schools, and your local woodworking or woodturning retailer. Many local woodturning clubs also have regular teaching demonstrations.

American Association of Woodturners
woodturner.org
75 5th St. W., 222 Landmark Center
St. Paul, MN 55102-7704
651-484-9094

Anderson Ranch Arts Center
andersonranch.org
P.O. Box 5598
Snowmass Village, CO 81615
970-923-3181

Arrowmont School of Arts and Crafts
arrowmont.org
P.O. Box 567
556 Parkway
Gatlinburg, TN 37738
865-436-5860

John C. Campbell Folk School
folkschool.org
One Folk School Rd.
Brasstown, NC 28902
800-365-5724

The Center for Art in Wood
centerforartinwood.org
141 N. 3rd St.
Philadelphia, PA 19106
215-923-8000

Center for Furniture Craftsmanship
woodschool.org
25 Mill St.
Rockport, ME 04856
207-594-5611

Center for Turning and Furniture Design
iup.edu/art/undergrad/studio/
    woodworking
Indiana University of Pennsylvania
Sprowls Hall (ground level)
470 S. 11th St.
Indiana, PA 15705
724-357-2538

Connecticut Valley School of Woodworking
schoolofwoodworking.com
249 Spencer St.
Manchester, CT 06040
860-647-0303

Conover Workshops
conoverworkshops.com
18115 Madison Rd.
P.O. Box 679
Parkman, OH 44080
440-346-3347

The Furniture Institute of Massachusetts
furnituremakingclasses.com
116 Water St.
Beverly, MA 01915
978-922-0615

Marc Adams School of Woodworking
marcadams.com
5504 E. 500 N.
Franklin, IN 46131
317-535-4013

David J. Marks Woodworking School
djmarks.com
2128 Marsh Rd.
Santa Rosa, CA 95403
707-526-6280

North House Folk School
northhouse.org
PO Box 759/500 Hwy 61 W
Grand Marais, MN 55604
218-387-9762

Peters Valley School of Craft
petersvalley.org
19 Kuhn Rd.
Layton, NJ 07851
973-948-5200

Port Townsend School of Woodworking
ptwoodschool.org
200 Battery Way
Port Townsend, WA 98368
360-344-4455

School of Art + Design
Purchase College, State University
    of New York
purchase.edu/departments/
    academicprograms/arts/artdesign
735 Anderson Hill Rd.
Purchase, NY 10577
914-251- 6750

Mark Supik Woodturning Workshops
marksupikco.com
1 N. Haven St.
Baltimore, MD 21224
410-732-8414

Vermont Woodworking School
vermontwoodworkingschool.com
148 Main St.
Cambridge, VT 05444
802-849-2013

Index

About the Author

David Heim grew up in Colorado and attended college in New York City. Although nominally an English major, he spent most of his time at the school's daily newspaper. After graduation he went on to earn a master's degree in journalism. For the next 28 years, David worked at *Consumer Reports* magazine, serving as its managing editor for much of that time. After leaving *Consumer Reports* in 2005, he became an associate editor at *Fine Woodworking* magazine and relocated to the small town of Oxford, Connecticut.

He now works as a freelance editor, writer, and designer, specializing in books and articles about woodturning and woodworking.

After learning the basics of woodturning from his father-in-law, David bought his first lathe in 2003 and began to make bowls. His shop now houses three lathes, including his father-in-law's Delta. You can see David's work on Etsy.com. He writes a regular column about woodturners and woodturning for the 360woodworking.com web site. In 2016, he was elected to the board of directors of the American Association of Woodturners.

IMPERIAL TO METRIC CONVERSION

Inches	mm*	Inches	mm*	Inches	mm*
1/32	0.79	17/32	13.49	2	50.8
3/64	1.19	35/64	13.89	3	76.2
1/16	1.59	9/16	14.29	4	101.6
5/64	1.98	37/64	14.68	5	127.0
3/32	2.38	19/32	15.08	6	152.4
7/64	2.78	39/64	15.48	7	177.8
1/8	3.18	5/8	15.88	8	203.2
9/64	3.57	41/64	16.27	9	228.6
5/32	3.97	21/32	16.67	10	254.0
11/64	4.37	43/64	17.07	11	279.4
3/16	4.76	11/16	17.46	12	304.8
13/64	5.16	45/64	17.86	13	330.2
7/32	5.56	23/32	18.26	14	355.6
15/64	5.95	47/64	18.65	15	381.0
1/4	6.35	3/4	19.05	16	406.4
17/64	6.75	49/64	19.45	17	431.8
9/32	7.14	25/32	19.84	18	457.2
19/64	7.54	51/64	20.24	19	482.6
5/16	7.94	13/16	20.64	20	508.0
21/64	8.33	53/64	21.03	21	533.4
11/32	8.73	27/32	21.43	22	558.8
23/64	9.13	55/64	21.83	23	584.2
3/8	9.53	7/8	22.23	24	609.6
25/64	9.92	57/64	22.64	25	635.0
13/32	10.32	29/32	23.02	26	660.4
27/64	10.72	59/64	23.42	27	685.8
7/16	11.11	15/16	23.81	28	711.2
29/64	11.51	61/64	24.21	29	736.6
31/64	11.91	31/32	24.61	30	762.0
1/2	12.70	63/64	25.00	31	787.4
33/64	13.10	1 inch	25.40	32	812.8

*Rounded to nearest 0.01 mm

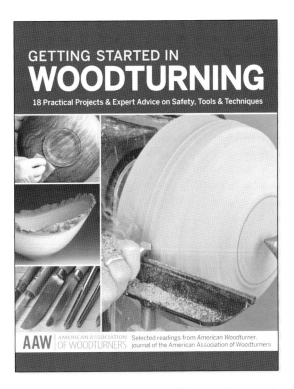

MORE GREAT BOOKS *from*
SPRING HOUSE PRESS

The Handmade Skateboard
978-1-940611-06-8
$24.95 | 160 Pages

Classic Wooden Toys
978-1-940611-34-1
$24.95 | 176 Pages

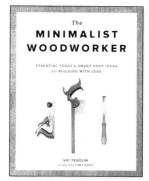

The Minimalist Woodworker
978-1-940611-35-8
$24.95 | 152 Pages

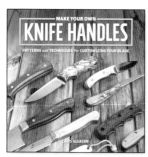

Make Your Own Knife Handles
978-1-940611-53-2
$22.95 | 144 Pages

The New Bandsaw Box Book
978-1-940611-32-7
$19.95 | 120 Pages

Make Your Own Cutting Boards
978-1-940611-45-7
$22.95 | 168 Pages

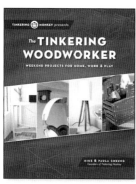

The Tinkering Woodworker
978-1-940611-08-2
$24.95 | 152 Pages

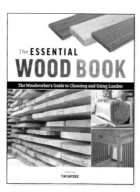

The Essential Wood Book
978-1940611-37-2
$27.95 | 216 Pages

The Essential Woodturner
978-1-940611-47-1
$27.95 | 228 Pages

SPRING HOUSE PRESS

Look for these Spring House Press titles at your favorite bookstore, specialty retailer, or visit *www.springhousepress.com*.
For more information about Spring House Press, call 717-208-3739 or email us at *info@springhousepress.com*.